글로벌셰프를 꿈꾸는 당신을 위한 필수 실무영어 !

Global Practical English for Culinary Arts

글로벌조리실무영어

고범석 · 김민영 · 나태균 공저

머리말

세계 외식시장의 규모는 약 5,000조 원에 달하고 있다. 사람들은 세계 각국의 음식 맛과 분위기에 열광하고 있으며, 음식을 통해 타국의 문화를 즐기는 시대에 접어들었다. 한국의 외식시장도 크게 변화하여 다양한 외국의 음식문화를 쉽게 즐길 수 있게 되었으며, 이에 따라 외국 요리를 배우기 위해 유학을 떠나거나 실무를 쌓기 위해 해외로 나가는 사례가 늘고 있다. 또한 한국 드라마의 붐으로 시작된 한류는 K-Pop을 통해 세계적인 관심을 받고 있으며, 이로 인해 한식에 대한 관심과 인기도 높아지면서 한식은 주요한 관광자원이 되었고, 해외 한식 레스토랑 수도 증가하고 있다. 그러나 선뜻 외국행을 결정하기 힘든 이유는 바로 언어라는 큰 장벽 때문이다.

이제 해외로 진출하려는 조리사 수는 많아지고 있으나, 이와 관련된 외국어 지침서가 매우 부족한 것 또한 사실이다. 또한 국내에서의 실무경험이 풍부하고 언어숙련도가 높다고 해도 해외에서 사용하는 식자재와 음식문화의 차이에 대한 정보는 여전히 부족한 형편이므로 이에 작은 도움이라도 되고자 본서를 집필하게 되었다.

본서는 해외 인턴십 업체와 외식분야에서 해외 경험이 풍부한 이들의 조언에 기초하여 필요한 내용을 4개의 핵심영역으로 나누어 다음과 같이 구성하였다.

PART I은 필자의 경험을 살려 주방에서 자주 사용되는 상황영어를 시작으로 레시피 영작연습과 조리용어 퍼즐을 통해 조리용어 및 필수 단어를 광범위하게 선별하여 기본회화에 익숙해지도록 구성하였다.

PART II는 식품 및 조리기구 용어를 바탕으로 만든 실전회화 영역이다. 원어로 된 식품, 음료, 조리기구, 주방기구에 대한 이해를 돕기 위해 사진을 넣었으며, 주방에서 사용 빈도가 높은 용어들을 선별하여 상황에 맞는 형식의 회화를 실었다. 또한 전 세계적으로 잘 알려진 영어 요리 레시피를 해석할 수 있도록 하였으며, 해외취업을 위한 면접 시에 한식을 영어로 소개하거나 외국인들에게 한식을 소개하기 위한 내용도 추가하였다.

PART Ⅲ는 영문법과 실용회화 영역으로 요리 영어에서 뼈대가 되는 가장 중요한 부분이라고 할 수 있다. 미국 등의 영어권 국가에 입국하는 과정과 그 후 그곳에서 주로 사용되는 실용회화 및 서식에 대한 표현사례를 실어 응용이 가능하도록 하였다.

PART Ⅳ는 해외취업 시 사용되는 영문 이력서 및 커버레터 작성법, 인터뷰방법, 취업정보 등을 실어 영문 서식에 대한 깊은 지식 없이도 조리사의 해외취업에 필요한 표현과 정보를 습득할 수 있도록 구성하였다.

부록에서는 메뉴작성에 필요한 전문조리용어와 식음재료 이동 인수증 및 창고물건불출증을 첨부하여 실무에서 사용되는 양식에 식자재주문 및 재료기입 작성 연습을 할 수 있도록 하였다.

이 책은 조리사의 해외취업이나 특급호텔 입성을 위해 정말 필요한 것이 무엇인가에 대한 핵심을 망라하고 있다. 막연히 소요되는 시간을 단축하고 방향을 알리기 위해 핵심만을 간추린 합리적이고 분별성 있는 조리영어 참고서이다.

가장 강력한 재테크는 시간이라고 한다. 조리를 공부하는 분들이 모쪼록 현실에 안주하지 말고 시간이라는 자원을 잘 활용하여 꾸준히 정진함으로써 모두들 최고가 되기를 바란다. 부족한 원고의 출판을 허락해 주신 백산출판사 진욱상 사장님과 직원 여러분, 그리고 늘 함께하시는 주님께 감사와 영광을 돌린다.

2014년
저자 일동

Contents

PART I

Chapter 1

조리 상황영어

상황영어 1

상황 1 : Cafe Kitchen (1)

 휴가를 다녀온 셰프. 휴가 중 바뀐 메뉴에 대해 대화하는 상황

셰프 : 좋은 아침이에요.

소영 : 안녕하세요, 셰프. 잘 쉬셨어요?

셰프 : 덕분에요.

셰프 : 냉장고에서 이상한 냄새가 나는 것 같아요. 그동안 청소 안 했어요?
　　　(다시 냉장고에 들어가서 상한 시금치를 꺼낸다) 이것 상했잖아요.

소영 : 예... 죄송합니다.

셰프 : 이것 쓰레기통에 갈아서 버려주세요.
　　　오늘 냉장고 들어내고 대청소합시다.

소영 : 예, 알겠습니다.

셰프 : 이번주에 스페셜 메뉴 바뀌었다면서요?

소영 : 예, 비프 웰링턴(beef wellington)으로요. 이번주부터 나가요.

셰프 : 웰링턴은 만들어 놓았나요?

소영 : 아니오. 총주방장님이 내일 아침에 만들라고 하셨어요.

셰프 : 그럼 파테 도우(pate dough)는 준비되었나요.

소영 : 예, 도우와 포스미트는 어제 만들어서 냉장고에 넣어 두었어요.

셰프 : 도우 녹여야 하니 꺼내주세요.

셰프 : 부처숍에서 안심은 타왔나요?

소영 : 예, 점심에 사용될 것 20개 주문은 해놓았어요.

셰프 : 소스는 어떻게 만들라고 했어요?

소영 : 양송이 소스인데요. 그리고요 총주방장께서 접시 바닥에 소스 뿌린 후, 웰링턴을 얹으
　　　라고 하셨어요. 그리고 소스에 핫소스를 조금 섞으라고 하셨어요.

셰프 : 많이 바쁘겠는걸. 빨리 만들어야 하니 소영 씨, 냉장고에서 재료 좀 꺼내주세요.

소영 : 예, 알겠습니다.

(전화벨이 울린다)

셰프 : 소영 씨, 미안하지만 전화 좀 받아줘.

Situational English 1

1. At a Cafe Kitchen (1)

 A situation that a chef who came back from a holiday talks about the changed menu.

(Chef : C, **Soyoung** : S)

C : Good morning!

S : Good morning, Chef! Did you enjoy your vacation?

C : Yes, thank you!

C : I could sense a strange smell. Haven't you done any cleaning while I'm gone?
(He comes back with a bunch of spoiled spinach from the fridge) This is all rotten.

S : I'm sorry.

C : Throw away this in the trash bin.
Let's clean up today.

S : Yes, chef.

C : I heard that the special menu has been changed.

S : Yes, it has. Beef Wellington from this week, chef.

C : Have you made Beef Wellington?

S : No, Executive Chef told us to make it tomorrow morning.

C : All right. Is the pate dough ready, then?

S : Yes, dough and forcemeat are made yesterday and kept in the fridge.

C : Okay, Take out the dough for defrosting.

C : What about the meat? Did you get the tenderloin from the butcher shop?

S : Yes, I ordered 20 ea. for lunch.

C : Did you get instructions for sauce?

S : Well, it's a mushroom sauce. Executive Chef told us to spread sauce onto the bottom of the plate and put wellington on top of it... and add some hot sauce in the sauce.

C : We're going to get quite busy. Let's hurry up. Take out the ingredients from the fridge.

S : Yes, chef!

(Telephone rings~~~)

C : Get the phone, please!

상황영어 2

 카페 주방에서 조리사들이 소영에게 조식 준비하는 것을 가르치는 상황

셰프 : 소영 씨, 주방에 랩이 하나도 없네! 창고물건불출증에 주문해 놓았어. 총주방장님에게
　　　사인 받아 창고 좀 다녀와요.
소영 : 예, 알겠습니다.

셰프 : 소영 씨, 달걀은 매일 30판씩 깨야 하니 냉장고에서 달걀 꺼내와요.
　　　그리고 모두 깨서 이 통에 담아요.
소영 : 예, 알겠습니다.
셰프 : 나중에 껍질은 체로 걸러내야 해요.

셰프 : 소영 씨, 프렌치토스트 할 것 제과주방 가서 식빵 10봉 타주세요.
소영 : 예, 알겠습니다.
셰프 : 소영 씨, 제과주방 갈 때 볼오방(vol-au-vent)도 같이 가져와요.
소영 : 예, 알겠습니다.

셰프 : 소영 씨, 달걀 스테이션에 콘디멘트 준비되었어요? 어제 남은 거 쓰면 안 되나요?
소영 : 토마토하고 치즈 조금씩 썰면 될 것 같아요.

소영 : 셰프, 여기 식빵 가져왔습니다.
셰프 : 냉장고 넣어 놓고 냉동실 들어가서 해시 브라운 감자 몇 판 있는지 확인해 주세요.
소영 : 3판 있습니다.
셰프 : 스튜어드에 가서 호텔 팬 큰 사이즈로 3개만 가져다주세요.
소영 : 호텔 팬은 하나도 없던데요.
셰프 : 그럼, 냉장고에 감자 담겨 있는 것 비우고 그것을 가져다주세요.
소영 : 예, 알겠습니다.
셰프 : 소영 씨, 해시 브라운 감자 만들어야 하니 감자를 스티머에 넣어주세요.
소영 : 몇 분 찔까요?
셰프 : 반만 익히고 15분 지나서 꼭 체크해야 해요!
소영 : 예, 알겠습니다.

셰프 : 여기 모두 모여보세요.
소영 : 예, 셰프님.
셰프 : 내일 아침 조식 예약 100명 늘었어요. 지금 준비한 것보다 2배로 준비해 주세요.
소영 : 예, 알겠습니다.

Situational English 2

 A situation that cooks are teaching Soyoung to prepare for breakfast in a cafe kitchen.

C : Soyoung, there's no wrap in the kitchen. I have put an order of store requisition. Get to the store after getting an approval from Executive Chef for that.
S : Yes, chef.

C : Soyoung, bring 30 trays of eggs from the fridge. Break them all and put it in here.
S : Yes, chef.
C : Remove the shell with a sieve.

C : Soyoung, go to the bakery kitchen and get 10 loafs of bread to make french toasts.
S : Yes, chef.
C : When you go to the bakery kitchen, bring the vol-au-vent with you.
S : Yes, chef.

C : Are you ready for condiments at the egg station? Can we use the leftover from yesterday?
S : I think we're set if we have a little of tomato and cheese.

S : Chef, here's the bread.
C : All right. Put them in the fridge and check how much potatoes we have for hash brown.
S : There are 3 pans.

C : Bring 3 hotel pans from the steward.
S : There's no pan left, chef.
C : If so, empty then pan with potatoes, and bring that one to me.
S : Yes, chef.
C : Put the potatoes into the steamer to make hash brown.
S : How long do we need to steam it?
C : Steam only the half. Make sure you check after 15 minutes.
S : Yes, chef.

C : Everyone, come here and listen up.
S : Yes, chef.
C : There is a reservation increase of 100 people for tomorrow morning breakfast. Double up what you have prepared.
S : Yes, chef.

상황영어 3

 가르드망제 주방에서 오르되브르 만들며 셰프와 조리사가 대화하는 상황

소영 : 셰프, 내일 칵테일파티 250명분 어떤 접시에 담아야 하지요?

셰프 : 훈제연어, 콜드 컷, 샌드위치, 스시네요. 사각접시에 3트레이씩 담아요.

소영 : 스시는 스테이션에서 만드나요?

셰프 : 아니요, 스시는 일식주방에서 만들어 올 거예요.
　　　부처숍에서 훈제연어, 콜드 컷 가져왔어요?

소영 : 지금은 준비 안됐다고 10시 이후에 오라고 하네요.

소영 : 샌드위치 빵은 냉장고에 넣어 두어야 잘 썰리니까 찬 것이 좋아요.

셰프 : 내일 파티용은 토스트해 주세요.

셰프 : 실습생에게 빵 토스트 시키세요.

소영 : 예, 알겠습니다.

셰프 : 소영 씨, 달걀노른자로 무스 좀 만드세요.

소영 : 어떻게 만들지요?

셰프 : 블렌더에 달걀노른자, 버터, 소금 넣고 갈아 체에 내리면 돼요.

소영 : 예, 알겠습니다.

셰프 : 오늘 들어온 허브가 별로 안 좋아요. 소영 씨, 허브 꺼내서 얼음물에 담가주세요.

소영 : 예, 알겠습니다.

셰프 : 카나페 다 만들었어요?

소영 : 예, 거의 다 만들어가요.

셰프 : 다 만들면 아스픽 처리해서 랩으로 싸주세요.

소영 : 예, 알겠습니다.

셰프 : 칼이 너무 안 드네요?

소영 : 어제 퇴근 전에 모두 갈아 놓은 건데요.

셰프 : 잘 안 갈렸어요. 다시 갈아야겠어요.

소영 : 예, 알겠습니다.

Situational English 3

 A conversation between a chef and a cook while making hors-d'oeuvre in Garde manger

S : Chef, what kind of plate do we need to use for the cocktail party tomorrow?

C : Well, we need smoked salmon, cold cuts, sandwiches, and sushi. Put them on 3 square plates.

S : Do we make a sushi at a sushi station?

C : No, they will make them from the Japanese kitchen.
    Did you bring smoked salmon and cold cuts from the butcher shop?

S : They asked me to come after 10:00am since they're not ready yet.

S : It slices well when the bread is cold. We'd better keep them in the fridge.

C : Toast the bread for the party tomorrow.

C : Let the trainee toast the bread.

S : Yes, chef.

C : Make some mousse with egg yolks.

S : How do you make it, chef?

C : Put egg yolks, butter and salt in a blender, and shift it.

S : All right, chef.

C : The herbs we have today are not very good. Put them in icy water.

S : Yes, chef.

C : Have you done with canapes?

S : Yes, almost ready.

C : When you're done with it, wrap it carefully.

S : Yes, chef.

C : Knives are dull.

S : Those have been sharpened before we went home last night.

C : Well, they don't work well, you'd better do it again.

S : Yes, chef.

상황영어 4

 이태리 주방에서 파스타를 만들며 셰프와 조리사가 대화하는 상황

소영 : 셰프, 카넬로니는 어떻게 만들어야 하지요?

셰프 : 지금부터 만들어야 하니 도와주세요.

소영 : 예, 알겠습니다.

셰프 : 일단 피망, 가지, 애호박, 버섯을 가지고 나와서 씻어요.

소영 : 예, 셰프.

셰프 : 나는 토마토소스를 끓일 테니 소영은 야채를 쥘리엔느로 썰어 소테해서 식혀요.

소영 : 예, 알겠습니다.

셰프 : 다 됐어요?

소영 : 예, 식으라고 냉장고에 넣어 두었어요.

셰프 : 잘했어요. 그럼 카넬로니 반죽 위에 그것을 올려서 말아주세요.

소영 : 몇 개나 만들죠?

셰프 : (오늘 예약이 별로 없으니...), 일인분에 2개씩 30개만 만들어요.

소영 : 예, 알겠습니다.

(12시 : 레스토랑 오픈)

셰프 : 주문 들어왔어요. 카넬로니 2개! 해산물 파스타 2개!
　　　 손님이 홍합 알레르기가 있다네요. 해산물 파스타에 홍합은 빼주세요.

소영 : 예, 셰프.

셰프 : 미스터 김이 카넬로니 만들어요. 그라탱 접시 바닥에 토마토소스 깔고 카넬로니 2개
　　　 올리고 소스, 치즈 뿌려서 오븐에 넣어요. 알겠지요?

소영 : 그런데 몇 도 정도로 구울까요?

셰프 : 200도 온도에 넣고 5~6분 후에 체크해요.

소영 : 예, 알겠습니다.

미국 주방에서 사용하는 언어	
Check the score	준비해야 할 음식 수를 알려주세요.
Draging	주문 음식 중 뭔가가 아직 준비되지 않아 못 나가고 있어요.
Drop	요리를 시작하세요.
Fire	요리를 긴급하게 만들어야 하는 상황
Get me a runner	지금 당장 이 음식을 테이블에 갖고 나갈 사람을 보내주세요.
Make it cry	양파를 추가해 주세요.
On a rail or on the fly	매우 급한 주문

출처 : 루이스 이구아라스 · 매튜 프레더릭, 요리학교에서 배운 101가지, 동녘, 2011, p. 5.

Situational English 4

4. At an Italian Kitchen

 A conversation between a chef and a cook in Italian kitchen making pasta

S : Chef, how do we make canelloni?

C : We're going to make it now, so help me, would you?

S : Yes, chef.

C : Please bring paprika, zucchini, and mushroom and wash them.

S : Yes, chef.

C : I'm going to make tomato sauce. Why don't you cut the vegetables in julienne? After that, saute and then cool it down.

S : Yes, chef.

C : Are you finished?

S : Yes, I put it in a fridge to chill it down.

C : Good job! Now, put it on canelloni dough and roll it up.

S : How many do we need today?

C : (We are not fully booked... so...) Make 30 of those, 2 for each serving.

S : Yes, chef.

(12:00 Noon Restaurant opens)

C : We have an order. Two Canelloni, and two seafood pasta! The customer is allergic to mussel. So take out the mussel from the seafood pasta.

S : Yes, chef.

C : Mr. Kim, make canelloni. Soyung, put tomato sauce on a gratin dish and put two canelloni, and then more sauce and cheese on top and then put it in an oven. Do you understand?

S : What should the temperature of the oven be?

C : Preheat 200℃ and check after 5-6 minutes.

S : Yes, chef.

상황영어 5

 셰프 미팅에서 총주방장과 각 부서의 주방장들이 함께 회의하는 상황

총주방장(EC) : 오늘 저녁 18시에 미 대사관에서 180명 세트메뉴 출장 있는데 메인이 등심에서 안심으로 변경되었습니다. 그리고 아스파라거스와 당근도 생으로 준비해주시고 고급 행사이니 차질 없도록 준비해 주세요.

최셰프 : 예, 알겠습니다.

총주방장(EC) : 각 부서에서 2명씩 지원해야 하니 지원자들은 17시에 연회주방으로 모여주시기 바랍니다.

셰프들(AC) : 예, 알겠습니다.

총주방장(EC) : 김 과장님, 오늘 점심 예약된 인원은 몇 명인가요?

김셰프(뷔페조리장) : 점심은 현재까지 150명으로 잡혀 있습니다.

총주방장(EC) : 김 과장님, 어제 저녁 때 보니 음식이 너무 많이 남았던데요?

김셰프(뷔페조리장) : 어제 예약이 250명이라 이에 맞춰 음식을 준비했는데, 50명 단체 예약이 갑자기 취소되어 그렇게 되었습니다.

총주방장(EC) : 알겠습니다.

총주방장(EC) : 이 과장님, 오늘 점심 예약된 인원은 몇 명인가요?

이셰프(일식조리장) : 점심 예약은 70명입니다.

총주방장(EC) : 삼정그룹 회장님과 친구분들 네 분 예약 있어요. 스페셜코스로 주문되어 있으니 특별히 신경 써주시고요. 양은 조금씩만 담아주시고 김 회장님이 송어회를 좋아하시니까 최고로 준비해 주시기 바랍니다.

그리고 이 과장님이 직접 나가서 회장님 맞으시고 음식 설명도 부탁합니다.

이셰프(일식조리장) : 예, 알겠습니다.

총주방장(EC) : 그리고 어제 뷔페음식에서 머리카락이 나와 컴플레인이 있었어요. 직원들 위생에 각별히 신경 써주시기 바라고 오늘도 수고해 주시기 바랍니다.

Situational English 5

A situation where the Executive Chef and chefs from all departments are having a meeting

(Executive Chef : EC, Chef Choi : CC, Chef Kim : CK, Chef Lee : CL, All Chefs : AC)

EC : It has been changed to tenderloin from sirloin for the outside catering of 180 people at a party in U.S. Embassy at 18:00 hours tonight. Please prepare asparagus and carrots in raw. Please take cautions as it is an important and high quality function.

CC : Yes, chef.

EC : We need two volunteers from each department and the volunteers are requested to be in banquet kitchen at 17:00 hours.

AC : Yes, chef.

EC : Chef Kim, how many do we have for lunch reservation today?

CK : For lunch, we have 150 people as of now.

EC : I saw that there was too much left over yesterday. What happened?

CK : We prepared food to meet for 250 people reserved but there was a last minute cancellation for the party of 50 people.

EC : All right.

EC : Chef Lee, how many do we have for lunch reservation today?

CL : We have 70 people reserved for lunch today.

EC : We have reservation of the chairman of Samjung and four of his friends. Please take a extra care as special course meals are ordered. Put only a small amount of food on each dish, and Chairman Kim prefers trouts for raw fish. Please do your very best to serve them.
Chef Lee, please greet and escort the chairman yourself and then explain about the food you prepare.

CL : Yes, chef.

EC : We have a complain that there was a strand of hair in the buffet food yesterday. Please make sure that all staff are requested to be careful with their personal hygienes. That's all for today. Thank you!

상황영어 6

 연회주방에서 케이터링 준비하는 상황

셰프 : 내일 그리스 대사관 100명분 바비큐 행사가 지금 들어왔어요. 소영이 맡아서 준비해 주세요.

소영 : 할 일도 많은데... 내일 몇 시 출발이지요?

셰프 : 12시 셋업이니 오전 9시에 출발해야 합니다.

소영 : 예, 알겠습니다.

소영 : (부처숍에 전화한다) 안녕하세요. 연회주방 미스터 김입니다.
　　　 내일 독일 대사관 출장행사가 있는데 미트로프하고 소시지 있어요?

부처 조리사 : 어떤 소시지요?

소영 : 세르블라 소시지와 초리조 소시지요.

부처 조리사 : 몇 개씩 필요하세요?

소영 : 각각 200개씩이요. 그리고 양갈비, 삼겹살, 닭다리도 10파운드씩 필요해요.

부처 조리사 : 예, 두 시간 후에 찾으러 오세요.

소영 : 알겠습니다.

셰프 : 부처숍 다녀올 때 스튜어드 가서 기물하고 케이터링 박스, 아트룸에 들러 드라이아 이스도 함께 가져오세요. 물건 들 때는 허리 조심하고...

소영 : 예, 알겠습니다.

(부처숍에 도착함)

부처 조리사 : 식재료이동영수증(inter-kitchen transfer) 가져왔어요? 잠깐만 기다리세요.
　　　 여기 미트로프, 소시지, 안심, 삼겹살, 양갈비, 드럼 스틱 모두 확인하세요.
　　　 맞지요?

소영 : 예, 고마워요. 수고하세요.

셰프 : 행사서(function sheet) 잘 체크해요. 그리고 기물 확인 잘해요.

소영 : 예, 알겠습니다.

Situational English 6

6. At a Banquet Kitchen (1)

 A situation to get ready for a outside catering

(Chef : C, **Soyoung** : **S**, Butcher : B)

C : We just have an order of barbeque party for outside catering at the Greek Embassy tomorrow. Soyoung, be in charge of all preparation for it.

S : I have a lot to do... When should we leave tomorrow?

C : We need to leave at 9:00 in the morning as the set up time is 12:00 o'clock.

S : Yes, chef.

(...calling the butcher shop)

S : This is Mr. Kim of banquet kitchen. We have an outside catering and do you have meat loafs and sausages?

B : What kind of sausages?

S : We need Cervelat and Chorizo sausages.

B : How many do you need each?

S : 200 of each. And we also need 10 pounds of lamb chop, pork belly, chicken drum stick each.

B : Okay, come and get after 2 hours.

S : Thank you!

C : When you go to the butcher shop, bring the necessary equipment from the steward, and dry ice from the artroom. And be careful with your waist when lifting a heavy stuff.

S : Yes, chef.

(Arriving at the butcher shop...)

B : Did you bring an inter-kitchen transfer? Okay, Just a second... Here are meat loaf, sausages, pork belly, lamb chop, drum stick. Make sure you have everything.

S : Yes, thank you!

C : Check the function sheet carefully. Also check the equipment.

S : Yes, chef.

상황영어 7

 연회주방에서 실습생으로 첫 출근한 상황

소영 : 안녕하세요.

셰프 : 이름이 어떻게 되지요?

소영 : 이소영이라고 합니다.

셰프 : 소영 씨! 반가워요.

셰프 : 일단 냉장고 들어가서 식재료의 위치를 파악하세요. 그리고 출근하면 행사지시서부터 확인해야 해요.

소영 : 예, 알겠습니다.

셰프 : 오늘 라자니아 만들어야 하니 베이커리 가서 도우 좀 밀어오세요.

소영 : 어떻게 하는지 잘 모르는데요?

셰프 : 걱정 마요. 오늘은 베이커리 직원이 가르쳐줄 거예요. 그리고 베이커리나 부처숍에 물건 받으러 갈 때에는 시트팬을 꼭 들고 가야 해요.

소영 : 예, 다녀오겠습니다.

(베이커리에서 도우를 가져옴)

셰프 : 여기 나무주걱으로 소스가 눋지 않게 중간에 한 번씩 저어주세요.

소영 : 셰프, 이 소스는 뭐죠?

셰프 : 이것은 미트소스, 이것은 베샤멜소스예요.

소영 : 예...

셰프 : 소영 씨, 유니폼이 더러워졌네요? 하우스키핑 가서 유니폼 갈아입고 행주 좀 타오세요.

소영 : 예, 셰프.

셰프 : 소영 씨, 여기 소스 좀 같이 들어요. 무거우니 허리 조심해요.
     하나, 둘, 셋!

셰프 : 됐어요. 이제 랩 씌우고 냉장고에 넣으세요.

소영 : 예, 셰프.

셰프 : 소영 씨, 오늘은 수고하셨고, 내일 아침 8시까지 출근하세요.

Situational English 7

7. At a Banquet Kitchen (2)

 A situation of the first day as a trainee

S : How are you? It's nice to meet you.
C : What is your name?
S : I'm Lee, Soyoung.
C : Nice to meet you, Soyoung.

C : First, go to the fridge and find out the location of ingredients. When you get to work.
S : Yes, chef.

C : Go to the bakery kitchen and spread dough to make lasagna today.
S : I'm not sure what to do with it.
C : Don't worry. Bakery staff will show you how to do it. Make sure you bring a sheet pan to get stuff from a bakery or butcher shop.

(Brought a dough)

C : Stir this sauce with a wooden ladle not to stick on a pot.
S : Chef, what is this sauce?
C : It's meat sauce. This is bechamel sauce....
S : Ah... yes.
C : Your uniform got dirty. Go to the housekeeping and get a new one. And get some dish cloth as well.
S : Yes, chef.

C : Soyoung, give me a hand to move the sauce. Be careful, it's heavy.
C : All right! Now, put a wrap and move it to the fridge.
S : Yes, chef.
C : That's all for today. Come back here at 8:00 tomorrow morning.

Chapter 2

조리단어와 레시피 영작

필수 조리동사

add	재료(양념)를 추가하다
blanch	데치다
blend	재료를 섞다
boil	끓이다
braise	노릇노릇하게 굽다, (고기, 채소 등을) 푹 삶다
broil	그릴(이나 오븐)에서 굽다
chop	~다지다
cube	깍둑썰기하다
deep fry	기름에 푹 담가서 프라이하다
drain	물기를 빼다
dry	말리다
flambe	불꽃으로 조리하다
grate	(치즈 등을) 갈다
grill	석쇠구이하다
marinate	밑간을 해서 재우다
melt	(버터 등을) 녹이다
mince	곱게 다지다
pan fry	기름을 두르고 프라이팬에서 전 부치듯이 조리하다
pour	(물/음료 등을) 붓다
preheat	(오븐이나 그릴을) 예열하다
rinse	헹구다
roast	오븐에서 굽다
saute	기름/물 등으로 볶다
season	양념하다
simmer	약한 불에 오랫동안 끓이다
slice	자르다
soak	불리다
spread	(버터, 소스 등을) 퍼 바르다
steam	찌다
stew	걸쭉하게 국처럼 끓이다
stir fry	빠른 시간에 휘저어 볶다

1. 레시피 영작해 보기

앞에서 익힌 조리 단어를 활용해서 아래 레시피를 해석해 봅시다.

Clam Chowder Soup
(Serving 8)

 Ingredients

3 (6.5 ounce) cans minced clams
1 cup minced onion
1 cup diced celery
2 cups cubed potatoes
1 cup diced carrots
3/4 cup butter
3/4 cup all-purpose flour
1 quart half-and-half cream
2 tablespoons red wine vinegar
1½ teaspoons salt
ground black pepper to taste

 **Direction**

❶ _____(물기를 빼다) juice from clams into a large skillet over the onions, celery, potatoes and carrots. Add water to cover, and cook over medium heat until tender.

❷ Meanwhile, in a large, heavy saucepan, _____(녹이다) the butter over medium heat. Whisk in flour until smooth. Whisk in cream and stir constantly until thick and smooth. _____(휘젓다) in vegetables and clam juice. Heat through, but do not boil.

❸ Stir in clams just before serving. If they cook too much they get tough. When clams are heated through, stir in vinegar, and _____(양념하다) with salt and pepper.

정답 ① Drain ② melt, Stir ③ season

Croque Monsieur
(Serving 4)

■ Ingredients

2 Tbsp butter
2 Tbsp flour
1½ cups milk
A pinch each of salt
freshly ground pepper, nutmeg, or more to taste
6 ounces Gruyere cheese, grated (about 1½ cups grated)
1/4 cup grated parmesan cheese (packed)
8 slices of French or Italian loaf bread
12 ounces ham, sliced
Dijon mustard

Direction

❶ _____(예열하다) oven to 400°F/200°C.

❷ Make the bechamel sauce. Melt butter in a small saucepan on medium/

low heat until it just starts to bubble. Add the flour and cook, stirring until smooth, about 2 minutes. Slowly _____(추가하다) the milk, whisking continuously, cooking until thick. Remove from heat. Add the salt, pepper, and nutmeg. Stir in the Parmesan and 1/4 cup of the grated Gruyere. Set aside.

❸ Lay out the bread slices on a baking sheet and toast them in the oven, a few minutes each side, until lightly toasted. For extra flavor you can _____(펴바르다) some butter on the bread slices before you toast them if you want.

(Alternatively, you can assemble the sandwiches as follows in step four and _____(석쇠구이하다) them on a skillet, finishing them in the broiler with the bechamel sauce.)

❹ Lightly _____(붓으로 펴바르다) half of the toasted slices with mustard. Add the ham slices and about 1 cup of the remaining Gruyere cheese. Top with the other toasted bread slices.

❺ Spoon on the bechamel sauce to the tops of the sandwiches. Sprinkle with the remaining Gruyere cheese. Place on a broiling pan. _____(오븐에서 굽다) in the oven for 5 minutes, then turn on the broiler and broil for an additional 3 to 5 minutes, until the cheese topping is bubbly and lightly browned.

If you top this sandwich with a fried egg it becomes a Croque Madame.

정답 ① Preheat ② add ③ spread, grill ④ brush ⑤ Roast

Japchae
(Serving 4-5)

Ingredients

8 ounces sweet potato noodles

1/2 bunch spinach (about 4 ounces), rinsed and trimmed

2 cloves garlic, minced

1 tablespoon plus 1½ teaspoons Asian sesame oil

1/4 teaspoon salt

1 tablespoon vegetable oil

6 ounces beef rib-eye, cut into 1/4- to

1/2-inch-thick strips

1/4 cup plus 1 teaspoon soy sauce

1/4 medium onion, sliced

3 to 4 pyogo or shiitake mushrooms, sliced

1 carrot, shredded or cut into thin strips

3 green onions, cut into 1-inch pieces

1/4 cup sugar

Toasted sesame seeds for garnish

Direction

❶ Cook the sweet potato noodles in a large pot of boiling water for 4 to 5 minutes. Immediately _____(물기를 빼다) and rinse thoroughly under cold water. Be sure not to overcook the noodles, or they will lose their chewy texture. If you like, cut the noodles with scissors into 6- to 7-inch lengths for easier eating.

❷ _____(데치다) the spinach in boiling water. _____(헹구다) immediately under cold water, squeeze the water from the leaves and form into a ball, and then cut the ball in half. Combine the spinach, half the garlic, 1/2 teaspoon of the sesame oil, and 1/4 teaspoon salt in a small bowl. Set aside to let the flavors soak in.

❸ _____(데우다) the vegetable oil in a large skillet over medium-high heat. Add the beef, the remaining garlic, 1 teaspoon of the soy sauce, and 1 teaspoon of the sesame oil. Stir-fry until the beef is cooked, 3 to 4 minutes. Add the onion, mushrooms, and carrot and cook until the onion is translucent, about 3 minutes. Add the green onions and stir-fry for another minute. Remove from the heat.

❹ In a large bowl, thoroughly _____(합하다) the noodles, beef mixture, spinach, remaining 1/4 cup soy sauce, 1 tablespoon sesame oil, and the sugar. Serve warm, sprinkled with sesame seeds.

① drain ② Blanch, Rinse ③ Heat ④ combine

Phat Thai
(Serving 4)

Ingredients

400g thick, dried, flat rice noodles (banh pho),
(we used Thai Taste rice noodles from Waitrose)
4 large garlic cloves, finely chopped
1 small bunch coriander, stems or roots
finely chopped, leaves reserved
50ml vegetable oil
200g raw prawns, peeled
85g pickled turnips, chopped (optional)
1 Tbsp sugar
3 eggs, beaten
2 Tbsp oyster sauce
2 Tbsp fish sauce
300g bean sprouts
juice 1 lime
1 bunch spring onions, sliced on the diagonal
100g roasted peanuts, crushed
3 red chillies, deseeded and finely chopped

 **Direction**

❶ _____(불리다) the noodles in cold water for up to 2 hrs., then drain and set aside. Using a pestle and mortar, pound the garlic with the chopped coriander stems or roots.

❷ Heat the oil in a wok over a high heat. When simmering, _____(추가하다) the garlic and coriander mix. _____ _____(기름을 두르고 휘젓다) for a few moments, then add the prawns and pickled turnip, if using. Cook for 30 secs., then add the sugar. Add the noodles and stir for 1 min, making sure everything is well mixed. Add the eggs and cook for 2 mins more.

❸ _____(붓다) in the oyster and fish sauce, then add the bean sprouts, lime juice, most of the spring onions, most of the roasted peanuts and most of the chilli. Toss and cook for around 2 mins, then serve scattered with coriander and the rest of the chilli, peanuts and spring onions.

정답 ① Soak ② add, Stir fry ③ Pour

Pizza Margherita
(Serving 2-3)

◼ Ingredients

12 inches thin pizza crust

(I use Boboli 12-inch thin crust)

1 tablespoon extra virgin olive oil

2 garlic cloves, finely chopped

3-4 large basil leaves, cut into strips

2 small tomatoes, cut thinly

4 ounces mozzarella cheese, shredded

2 tablespoons parmesan cheese

salt and pepper, to taste

Optional

crushed red pepper flakes, to taste

Direction

❶ _____(예열하다) the oven to 450˚F.

❷ Drizzle the olive oil over the pizza shell. Use a brush to spread it around and make sure to get the crust!

❸ Next, disperse the finely chopped garlic evenly.

❹ Spread the mozzarella cheese throughout the top, but keep it thin.

❺ Place the thinly sliced tomatoes across the entire pizza.

❻ Lightly salt and pepper the tomatoes with the kosher salt.

❼ _____(펴바르다) the fresh basil leaves, making sure to get some on tomatoes and on just the cheese itself.

❽ Cook the pizza in the oven for about 9–10 minutes, or until sufficiently crispy and melted to your liking.

❾ _____(추가하다) a little Parmesan cheese and (optional) crushed red pepper and enjoy!

Chapter 3

조리용어 퍼즐

1. 육류(Meats)

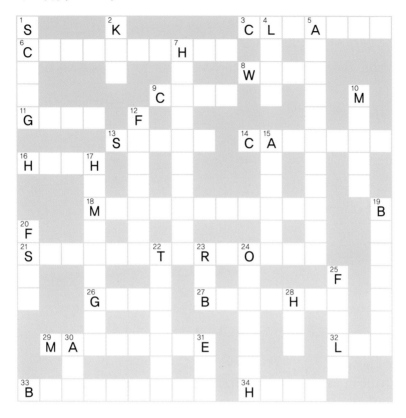

3. A butcher's knife having a large square blade

6. English breeds of domestic fowl often crossbred to produce roasters

8. Travel organ

9. Young of various large placental mammals
   e.g. whale or giraffe or elephant or buffalo

11. Animal hunted for food or sport

13. Cut

14. The stomach lining of pork which is used in place of back fat for pate and
   to encase crepinettes

16. Red flannel is one type

18. Sometimes served in school cafeterias or institutional dining rooms

21. Abattoir

26. Wild ox of moutainous areas of eastern India

27. Meatman

29. Frequently used to season meat

32. The back part of the hindquarter of a meat animal

33. A flat cut of beef, usually cut perpendicular to the muscle fibers. Beefsteaks are usually grilled, pan-fried, or broiled.

34. Fully or overly aged

DOWN

1. The lean end of a neck of veal

2. A young goat

4. A cut of meat taken from the side and back of an animal between the ribs and the rump

5. French : A long thin slice of poultry breast

7. Sausage or jellied loaf made of chopped parts of the head meat and sometimes feet and tongue of a calf or a pig

10. The flesh of animals used as food

12. German for 'meat'

15. A French lamb less than one year old

17. Quintessentially American, but could also be considered 19th century German or medieval Mongolian (related to 22 down)

19. Meat that is salted and cut into strips and dried in the sun. South African jerky

20. Service of the USDA that inspects livestock and carcasses for meat safety and wholesomeness

22. Medieval Mongolian steak (related to 17 down)

23. Spare

24. African ratite used for food

25. Manchette

28. Thigh of a hog

30. Maturate

31. Large North American deer with large much-branched altlers I the male

1 S		2 K				3 C	4 L	E	A	5 V	E	R
6 C	O	R	N	I	S	H	H	7 E	N		O		I
R		D		E		8 W	I	N	G		U		
A				9 C	A	L	F		N		I		10 M
11 G	A	M	E		12 F		D				I		E
		13 S	L	I	C	E		14 C	15 A	U	L	F	A	T
16 H	A	17 S	H		E		H		G		L		T
		A		I		H		N		E		S
		18 M	Y	S	T	E	R	Y	M	E	A	T		19 B
20 F		B		C		S		A		T			I
21 S	L	A	U	22 G	H	T	23 E	R	24 H	O	U	S	E		L
I		R		A		I		S		25 F		T
S		26 G	A	U	R		27 B	U	T	28 C	H	E	R		O
		E		T		R		A		I		N
	29 M	30 A	R	I	N	A	D	31 E		I		M	32 L	E	G
	G		R		L		C		L
33 B	E	E	F	S	T	E	A	K		34 H	I	G	H

2. 소스(Sauces)- I

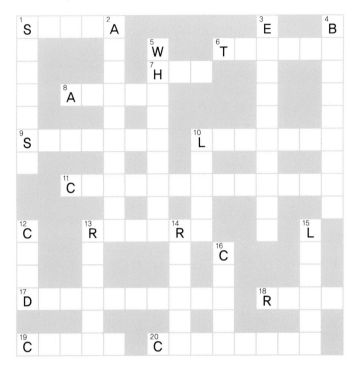

1. Tomato-based, hot sauces typical of Mexican cuisine, particularly those used as dips

6. Mildly acid red pulpy fruit eaten as a vegetable Italian sauce

7. Used physical heat; having a high or higher than desirable temperature or giving off heat or feeling or causing a sensation of heat or burning

8. Garlic mayonnaise

9. A French sauce made by adding cream to a veloute made from chicken stock.

10. A binding or thickening agent used in cooking

11. Liquid left after a food has beed cooked

13. A brown sauce spicy with mustard

17. Mustard flavored mayonnaise type sauce served with cold meats

18. A mixture of fat and flour heated and used as a basis for sauces

19. A dairy product that is composed of the higher-butterfat layer skimmed from the top of milk before homogenization

20. Many dishes are named after this Renaissance chateau

DOWN

1. A bechamel-based sauce containing strained or pureed onions

2. A soup or sauce made of chicken stock, rice, egg yolks, and lemon sauce

3. Blended by the suspending of small globules of one liquid (as oil) in another (as water or vinegar)

4. A thick sauce made from meat, vegetables, and tomatoes often finished with a little cream or milk

5. Sauce containing pale yellowish fermented grape juice

10. Not heavy

12. Having a low or inadequate temperature

13. Pepper sauce garnished with hard-cooked egg whites, mushrooms ox tongue and gherkins

14. Spicy or savory condiment

15. The state in which a substance exhibits a characteristic readiness to flow with little or no tendency to disperse and relatively high incompressibility

16. The part of milk containing the butterfat

3. 소스(Sauces)-Ⅱ

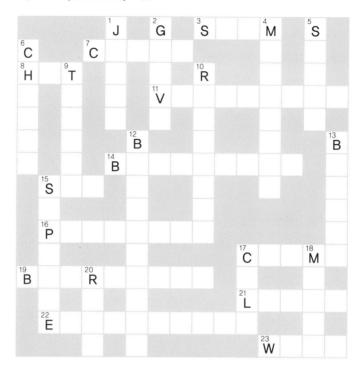

3. Remove from the surface of liquid

7. Season with a mixture of spices; typical of Indian cooking

8. Peppery

11. Baby beef broth

14. Meat and tomato sauce

15. A source of oil; used for forage and soil improvement and as food

16. Allemande sauce with chopped parsley

17. A dairy product that is composed of the higher-butterfat layer skimmed from the top of milk before homogenization

19. A sauce like hollandaise but made with white wine and tarragon and shallots instead of lemon juice

21. Not heavy

22. Cause to become an emulsion

23. Fermented juice

1. Made often from the juices that run naturally from meat or vegetables during cooking
2. A sauce made from meat juices
4. Orange Hollandaise
5. Having an agreeably pungent taste
6. Red Bearnaise
9. Midly acid red or yellow pulpy fruit eaten as a vegetable
10. Veloute sauce seasoned with herbs and shallot and capers
12. Brown sauce with beef marrow and red wine
13. Butter
15. A rich veloute made with chicken stock, cream and egg yolk
17. As mayonnaise, tartare, etc.
18. Possible origin of mayonnaise
20. A mixture of fat and flour and used as a basis for sause

해 답

4. 과일(Fruits)

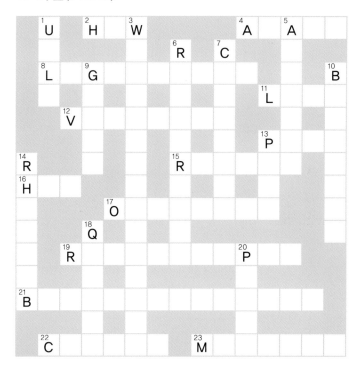

ACROSS

2. A spring flowering shrub or small tree of the genus crataegus

4. Tropical American plants with basal rosettes of fibrous sword-shaped leaves & flowers in tall spikes. Used in making alcoholic beverages

8. Cross between a blackberry & raspberry, developed in 1881 in Santa Cruz, California

11. Small tropical tree whose green fruit is rich in vitamin C; native to the Indonesian archipelago or nearby mainland Asia

12. A summer orange with thin, golden, hard to peel skin, not entirely seedless

13. A fleshy fruit (apple or pear or related fruits) having seed chambers and an outer fleshy part

15. A substance that curdles milk in making cheese and junket

16. The aggregate fruit of the rose plant

17. Any of several shrubs having silver-white twigs and yellow flowers followed by olivelike fruits

19. A winter apple with a rough reddish-brown skin

21. A large pippin apple, popular in early 19th century England

22. The fruit of many plants of the genus Prunes, and is a fleshy drupe (stone fruit)

23. Ground black cherry pits used as flavoring in the Middle East

DOWN

1. Large sweet juicy hybrid between tangerine and grapefruit

3. A russet colored pear, juicy & tender, keeps very well in cold storage

5. A sweet, thick-fleshed fruit that is often preserved in dried form

6. Small red berries used primarily in jams and jellies

7. Another name for the Brazil nut

9. A fruiting berry of the deciduous woody vines of the botanical genus *Vitis*

10. Seed of the Areca palm

13. Old World tree having sweet gritty-textured juicy fruit : widely cultivated in many varieties

14. Long pinkish sour leafstalks usually eaten cooked and sweetened

18. Small Asian tree with pinkish flowers and pear-shaped fruit; widely cultivated

20. Downy juicy fruit with sweet yellowish or whitish flesh

해 답

5. 음료(Beverages)

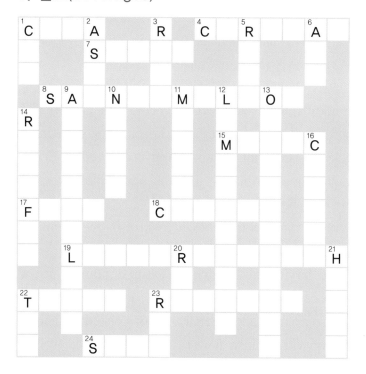

ACROSS

1. A carbonated beverage that originally contained caffeine from the kola nut and cocaine from coca leaves and was flavored with vanilla and other ingredients
5. Wines that are not effervescent
7. Bottom fermented beer stored at low temperature for a period of time
10. A beverage believed to cure all ills
11. Thin syrup made from pomegranate juice
12. An old name for a strong ale
14. Any of various strong liquors distilled from the fermented sap of toddy palms or from fermented molasses
15. Fermented juice
18. Fermented beverage heavier than beer
19. Originally, water from Nieder Selters, Germany
20. _____ Whiskey
23. Rum and lime or lemon juice with sugar and sometimes bitters
24. Unfermented grape juice

DOWN

1. Red Burgundy wine from Cote de Beaune; favorite of Louis XI
2. One of the ingredients of the original martini
3. A liqueur made with gin and the sour fruit of the blackthorn
4. Darjeeling, Assam, and Travancore and 3 examples
6. Made from white grapes or red grapes with skin removed
8. The last ingredient in a Moscow Mule
9. A light pink wine, usually best when young and drunk cool
13. A full flavored gin with a malty flavor and aroma; Dutch gin
16. A city of northwest Italy southeast of Turin noted for its sparkling wines
17. A fortified desserts wine made on an island off Portugal
21. An illicitly distilled alcoholic liquor
22. Distilled from fermented molasses
23. Liquor distilled from fermented Molasses

해 답

6. 수프(Soups)

ACROSS

5. Soup station chef in brigade system

6. English potage

7. Solanum tuberosum potage. Using the potato potage

9. Turkish soup of beef stock & small meat-filled dumplings, garnished with yogurt, thyme and mint

10. A French dish which provides at the same time soup, boiled meat and vegetables

12. A thick soup made of dried peas

13. Swedish yellow split pea soup eaten on Thursday

15. Classic Arab food staples that consist of barbecued meat and poultry such as kebab and shish taouk

16. Mussel soup probably created at Maxim's for William B. Leeds

17. Sometimes added to bisques at the table

18. (Spanish) Soup

DOWN

1. (French) Thick hearty soup that is similar to stew with chunks of garnish

2. German cabbage soup with meat stock, meat and vegetables

3. Soup with coincidental link to Yale University

4. One Italian word for soup

5. What Vichyssoise really is : cold...

8. Norwegian soup made with milk, rice, lemon peel & milk beer flavored with sugar

11. Broken dried Jewish noodles for soup

14. Hawaiian noodle soup

16. Alcoholic beverage sometimes paired with cheese in soups

해 답

S						K			B	Z
O	P	O	T	A	G	E	R		O	U
U	O					A		S	O	U	P
P	O	T	A	T	O	S	O	U	P	L	P
E	A		L		T		A	D	A	N	A
	T		S		S		B				
P	O	T	A	U	F	E	U	F	O	
	L		P		P	E	A	S	O	U	P
	E		P		P		R	L		
A	E	R	T	E	R	M	E	D	F	L	A	S	K
K						E		A	
M	A	S	H	A	W	I	B	I	L	I	B	I
	O				E		M	
	U		S	H	E	R	R	Y	I	
S	O	P	A		R		N	

7. 향신료(Herbs & Spices)

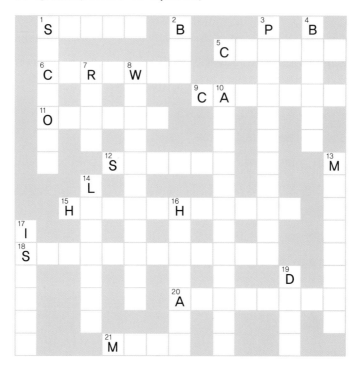

ACROSS

1. Any of various plants of genus Cassia, with showy, nearly regular, usually yellow flowers, Many are used medicinally, and seeds of some species are used as coffee substitute in various parts of the world

5. The aromatic dried flower buds of a tree

6. Seedlike fruit of a biennial Eurasian herb in parsley family, with finely divided leaves and clusters of small, white or pinkish flowers

9. Hairy aromatic perennial herb having whorls of small white purple-spotted flowers in a terminal spike, used in the past as a domestic remedy, strongly attactive to cats

11. Perennial northern temperate plant with toothed leaves and heads of small purplish-white flowers. Also called live-forever

12. East Indian annual erect herb; source of sesame seed or benniseed and sesame oil

15. Any of various plants of the genus Gratiola, growing in damp places and having small yellow or whitish flowers. Honey from these plants is particularly good

18. Shrubby European wormwood naturalized in North America, sometimes used in brewing beer

20. Any of various herbs in the parsley family, having small white or greenish flowers in compound umbels, whose roots and fruits are used in flavoring liqueurs and whose stems are candied and eaten

21. Spice made from dried fleshy covering of the nutmeg seed

DOWN

1. Chicory, alternate name

2. Small Mediterranean evergreen tree with small blackish berries and glossy aromatic leaves used for flavoring in cooking; also used by ancient Greeks to crown victors

3. The scientific name come from the 'calendula'

4. Avens of Virginia having pale or greenish yellow flowers

7. Source of Canola oil

8. Checkerberry

10. Ferns with fertile spikes shaped likes a snake's tongue

13. A purple flowered Mediterranean plant whose sweet-smelling leaves are used to season food

14. Leaves of any of various plants of Lactucasativa

16. Poisonous fetid Old World plant in the mustard family, formerly cultivated for its leaves that yield a blue dye

17. Old world genus of annual of perennial herbs

19. Aromatic old world herb having aromatic threadlike foliage and seeds used as seasoning

해 답

¹S	E	N	N	A		²B			³P		⁴B		
U						A	⁵C	L	O	V	E	S	
⁶C	A	R	⁷A	W	⁸A	Y			T		N		
C		A		I		⁹C	¹⁰A	T	M	I	N	T	
¹¹O	R	P	I	N	E				A		E		
R		E		T			D		R		T		
Y		¹²S	E	S	A	M	E		I			¹³M	
	¹⁴L		R				R		G			A	
¹⁵H	E	D	G	E	¹⁶H	Y	S	S	O	P		R	
¹⁷I		T		R		E		T		L		J	
¹⁸S	O	U	T	H	E	R	N	W	O	O	D	O	
A		U		E		B		N		¹⁹D		R	
T		C		N	²⁰A	N	G	E	L	I	C	A	
I		E		N				U		L		M	
S		²¹M	A	C	E			E		L			

8. 조리기구(Cooking Tools & Equipments)

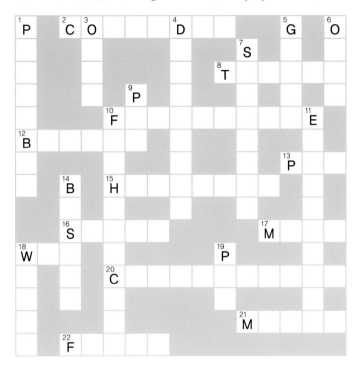

2. A type of strainer that is perforated utensil for washing or draining food

8. A traditional shallow earthenware Moroccan cooking pot with a conical lid

10. A long deep cooking container with two handles, a grid, and a lid

12. A physical feature sometimes needed to cook foods with charcoal or wood

13. Cooking utensil consisting of a wide metal vessel

15. A rectangular stainless steel pan with a lip, usual size is 12×20 inches

16. One of the oldest utensils

17. Necessary to make stilton cheese

18. Pan with a convex bottom, used for frying in certain countries

20. Used to cook semolina in North Africa

21. An appliance used in breadmaking

22. Italian and Portuguese for oven

1. A cabinet designed for professional bakers, is the final dough-rise step before baking, and refers to a specific rest period within the more generalized process known as fermentation
3. An earthenware pot used to cook stews in Spain, Central & South America
4. Iron or earthenware cooking pot; used for stews
5. A framework of mental bars used as a partition or a grate
6. Kitchen appliance used for baking or roasting
7. A round shallow pan with straight of flared sides and a handle
9. The single, central kernel or stone of certain fruits
10. A long narrow, metal pan with a perforated rack used to raise and lower fish in one piece
11. Metal or pottery which has been overlayed with a hard, glassy substance
14. Can be made from flexible vegetables fibers
18. A mixer incorporating a coil of wires
19. Metal or earthenware cooking vessel that is usually round and deep; often has a handle and lid

해 답

9. 종합 테스트(Final Test)

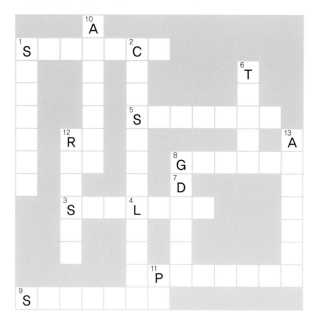

1. A vegetable with large dark green leaves that were originated from Southeast of Asia.

3. A good quality piece of beef which is cut from the lower part of a cow's back. It is usually cooked as a steak.

5. A bright yellow spice that is used in cooking to give food a special taste and colour originated from southern Europe and Asia Minor. It is sold as a powder or in thin pieces.

8. A tool used for breaking into small pieces of food

9. A tool used to remove something from the surface of a liquid, especially floating fat, solids, or oil.

11. A red powder made from a type of sweet pepper, used for giving a slightly hot taste to meat and other food.

DOWN

1. A small sea creature that you can eat, with a flat round shell made of two parts

that fit together. It can be roasted or steamed.

2. The French word for watercress that is usually used for appetizer or salads (7 letters)

4. A large deep spoon with a long handle, used for lifting liquid food, especially soup, out of a container (5 letters)

6. A common river-fish colored orange, often used for food, or the flesh of this fish.

7. A type of herb that is similar to caraway in the form and taste. It is a green herb with wiry, thread-like leaves that grow in clusters. It has a strong, distinctive taste that is like a combination of fennel, anise and celery, with warm, slightly bitter undertones. (4 letters)

10. A very small fish that tastes strongly of salt. It usually comes in the form of canned food.

12. A dried grape

13. An aromatic green vegetable. It is also known as rocket, roquette, arugula and rucola, and is popular in Italian cuisine.

해 답

Chapter **4**

실무 필수회화

번호	회 화
1	달걀 모자라지 않나요? Aren't we short of eggs?
2	나는 ○○가 필요합니다. I need ○○.
3	이것을 씻어주실래요? Can you wash this?
4	아주 급한 주문이에요. It's an urgent order.
5	제 실수에 대해 사과드립니다. I am sorry for my mistake.
6	곧 가서 가져오겠습니다. I will go and get it right away.
7	실례하지만 다시 한 번 말씀해 주시겠습니까? Pardon me. Could you please go over it again?
8	잠시 후에 도와드리겠습니다. I'll be with you in a moment.
9	물론이죠. 제가 해드리겠습니다. Yes, certainly. Allow me.
10	방해해서 죄송합니다. Excuse me for interrupting.
11	계란을 어떻게 해드릴까요? How would you like your eggs?
12	도와주시겠습니까? Could you help me, please?

번호	회 화
13	이 정도면 충분합니까, 셰프님? Is this enough, chef?
14	드셔보세요. 맛있습니다. Try it, It's very tasty.
15	얼마만큼 드릴까요? How much would you like?
16	어떤 것부터 도와드릴까요? What can I help you with first?
17	이것은 어떻게 만듭니까? How do you cook this?
18	좋은 생각이 있습니다. I've got an idea.
19	스토브에 물 좀 올려주세요. Put some water on the stove.
20	잠시 휴식을 합시다. Let's take a break.
21	당신에게 달렸습니다. It's up to you.
22	소금을 너무 많이 넣었습니다. We put too much salt.
23	일을 서둘러야 합니다. We need to work fast.
24	맛을 보시겠습니까? Could you taste this?
25	너무 짭니까? Is it too salty?

번호	회 화
1	셰프와 이야기할 수 있을까요? May I speak to the chef?
2	다음에 하면 어떨까요? Could we make it some other time?
3	제 사과를 받아주십시오. Please accept my apologies.
4	밀가루를 더 넣어야 합니다. We need to add some more flour.
5	누가 이 음식을 준비했나요? Who prepared this dish?
6	이 요리는 양파와 마늘을 충분히 볶아야 해요. Onions and garlics should be sauteed throughly.
7	기다리시게 해서 죄송합니다. I'm sorry to have kept you waiting.
8	서두르시지 않아도 됩니다. Please take your time. There is no hurry.
9	천천히 하십시오(서두르지 마십시오). Take your time, please. There is no hurry.
10	어떤 것을 드릴까요? 이것 아니면 저것을 드릴까요? Which one do you prefer, this or that one?
11	이 소스에 등심을 절여야지요. Sirloin should be marinated with this sauce.
12	당근은 너무 크게 썰지 말아요. Do not cut the carrot in big sizes.

번호	회 화
13	저는 괜찮습니다. I have no problem with it.
14	제안이 있습니까? Are there any suggestions?
15	우선 무엇부터 도와드릴 수 있을까요? What should I help you with first?
16	주문이 많이 들어왔습니다. There are a lot of orders.
17	이 시간에는 매우 바쁩니다. We are very busy at this time.
18	조심하십시오. 뜨겁습니다. Be careful, it's very hot.
19	손님들이 기다리십니다. The guests are waiting.
20	어떻게 생각하십니까? What do you think of it?
21	조리법을 알려주십시오. Could you give me the recipe?
22	냉장고에서 ○○를 꺼내주세요. Take ○○ out from the fridge.
23	수프는 식혀야 하니 한 번씩 저어주세요. Stir the soup to cool it off.
24	죄송합니다. 이해가 안되는데 셰프를 불러 드리겠습니다. I'm sorry. I don't understand. I'll get the chef for you.
25	첫 모퉁이에서 왼쪽/오른쪽으로 돌아가십시오. Turn left / right at the first corner.

번호	회 화
1	점심 예약이 몇 명인가요? How many tables do we have for lunch?
2	지금은 시간이 안됩니다. I don't have the time at the moment.
3	크림을 소스에 왜 넣지 않았습니까? Why didn't you put creme in the sauce?
4	상황에 따라 다릅니다. It depends on the given situation.
5	당신이 결정해 주셨으면 합니다. I'd like you to make the decision.
6	이쪽으로 와주시겠어요? Would you please come this way?
7	잠시 기다리시면 제가 알아봐 드리겠습니다. Please wait a moment. I'll check it for you.
8	상의할 것이 있습니다. There's something I'd like to discuss with you.
9	아무 소스나 저는 괜찮습니다. Whichever sauce you decide is all right with me.
10	Lobster bisque soup는 어떻게 만듭니까? How do you make lobster bisque?
11	죄송하지만 현재는 이것밖에 생각해 낼 수 없습니다. I'm sorry, but that's all I can think of at the moment.
12	소스가 다 떨어졌습니다. We are run out of sauce.

번호	회 화
13	후식으로 아이스크림을 드시겠습니까? Would you like to have some ice cream for dessert?
14	스테이크는 어느 정도로 구울까요? How would you like your steak?
15	남은 음식은 반드시 랩을 씌워주세요. Left overs should be wrapped.
16	최고의 요리사에게 소개해 드리겠습니다. Let me introduce you to a great chef.
17	요리가 마르니 후드 커버로 덮어 놓으세요. Cover the dish to keep from drying up.
18	등심(sirloin steak)은 미디엄 레어로 구우세요. Cook the sirloin steak medium rare.
19	식사를 잘 하셨습니까? Did you enjoy your meal?
20	불을 너무 세게 하지 마세요. Do not set the flame too high.
21	잠시 말씀드려도 될까요? May I speak to you for a moment?
22	미즈 앙 플라스(mise en place) 다시 한 번 확인하세요. Check mise en place again.
23	내일 몇 시까지 출근해야 하죠? What time should I report to work tomorrow?
24	이것 깨끗하게 닦으세요. Clean up this thoroughly.
25	시장에서 가져온 싱싱한 전복이 있습니다. We have fresh abalone from the market.

번호	회 화
1	베이글 샌드위치가 맛있다고 조리법을 알려달라고 합니다. He says that bagel sandwich is delicious and that he'd like to have the recipe.
2	음식 식어요! 지금 바로 이 음식이 30번 테이블에 나가야 돼요. Food is getting cold. This should go to table 30 right now!
3	알려주셔서 감사합니다. Thank you for bringing the matter to our attention.
4	대단히 죄송합니다. 문제가 있었던 것 같습니다. I am terribly sorry. There must have been a mistake.
5	알려주셨더라면 즉시 조치해 드릴 수 있었을 텐데요. I do wish you had let us know earlier. We could have put things right immediately.
6	죄송하지만 규칙에 어긋납니다. I'm so sorry we can't do that. It's against our rules/policy.
7	죄송하지만 저희가 하지 못하도록 되어 있습니다. I'm terrible sorry. We are not permitted to do this.
8	스톡에 사용될 닭뼈를 부처에서 가져왔나요? Did you bring the chicken bones for stock from the butcher shop?
9	제 결정에 달린 것은 알지만 다른 의견도 듣고 싶습니다. I know it's up to me, but I'm open to other suggestions.
10	좋아요! 저도 역시 그 소스를 선택했을 것입니다. Good! That's the sauce I'd have picked anyway.
11	이 드레싱은 야채를 블렌더에 넣어 곱게 갈아야 해요. Vegetables should be ground finely in a blender for this dressing.
12	저녁에 사용할 닭다리를 소스에 재워 놓았나요? Are chicken legs for the dinner menu marinated in the sauce?

번호	회 화
13	메인요리가 나오기 전에 전채를 드시겠습니까? Would you care for an appetizer before the main dish?
14	죄송하지만 확실하지 않습니다. 잠시만 기다리신다면 알아봐 드리겠습니다. I'm sorry. I'm not sure. If you'll wait for a minute, I'll be glad to find out for you.
15	○○ 레스토랑을 추천해 드리고 싶습니다. 음식이 매우 좋습니다. I suggest the ○○ restaurant. The food there is great.
16	오븐 온도는 몇 도로 맞출까요, 셰프? What temperature should the oven to be set, chef?
17	저 코너에는 찬 음식이 준비되어 있습니다. There are cold food in that corner.
18	네, 제가 000입니다. 어떻게 도와드릴까요? Yes, I am 00. How can I help you?
19	오늘 위생검열이 있어요. 냉장고 깨끗하게 청소해야 하고 유통기한 체크해야 합니다. We have a kitchen hygiene check-up today. We need to clean up the refrigerators and check the expiration dates for food.
20	고추가 매우니 조금씩만 사용하세요. Use a little bit of pepper because it's hot.
21	재고가 많이 있으니 빨리 사용하세요. Use up the ingredients as we have a lot of them in stock.
22	죄송합니다. 문제가 있었던 것 같은데 사과드립니다. I'm terrible sorry. There must have been some mistakes. I do apologize.
23	외국손님들에게는 아마도 김치가 가장 인기 있을 것입니다. I'll bet the Kimchi is the favorite for most foreigners.
24	기름온도가 너무 높아요. 불 줄이세요. The oil temperature is too high. Lower it down.
25	어제 가져온 연어가 상한 것 같아요. The salmon we brought yesterday is not quite fresh.

PART Ⅱ

Chapter **1**

식재료와 조리기구의 용어 및 회화

1. 과일류

키위 Kiwi	파파야 Papaya	붉은 포도 Red Grape	청포도 Green Grape
캠벨포도 Campbell	크리스핀(사과) Crispin	매킨토시(사과) Mcintosh	브레이번(사과) Braeburn
엠파이어(사과) Empire	갈라(사과) Gala	그래니스미스(사과) Granny Smith	골든 딜리셔스(사과) Golden Delicious
렉스톤스 수펄브(사과) Laxton's Superb	에그리맨 러싯(사과) Egremont Russet	콕스 오렌지 피핀(사과) Cox's Orange Pippin	롬 뷰티(사과) Rome Beauty
브램리(사과) Bramley's Seedling	레드 딜리셔스(사과) Red Delicious	오를레앙 레네트(사과) Oreleans Reinette	큰 야생능금(사과) Large Crabapple

1) 과일명이 쓰이는 주방 실무회화

❶ 소영 씨, 사과는 큐브로 써세요.

→ Soyoung, cut the apples in cubes.

（응용） Cut the macintosh in dice.

❷ 소영 씨, 냉장고 들어가서 골든 딜리셔스 사과 2개만 꺼내주세요.

→ Soyoung, get me two golden delicious apples from the refrigerator.

（응용） Get me three eggs from the fridge.

❸ 소영 씨, 사과가 몇 종류나 있는지 알아요?

→ Soyoung, do you know how many kinds of apples there are?

（응용） Do you know how many kinds of melons there are?

❹ 소영 씨, 립 아이 스테이크 마리네이드 소스에 키위 한 개만 갈아 넣어요.

→ Soyoung, put just one ground kiwi in the marinated sauce for rib eye steak.

（응용） Marinate the beef in the garlic sauce.

❺ 소영 씨, 요즘 브레이번이 샐러드 만들기에 적합해요.

→ Braeburns are great for salad these days.

（응용） Red delicious are great for apple pies these days.

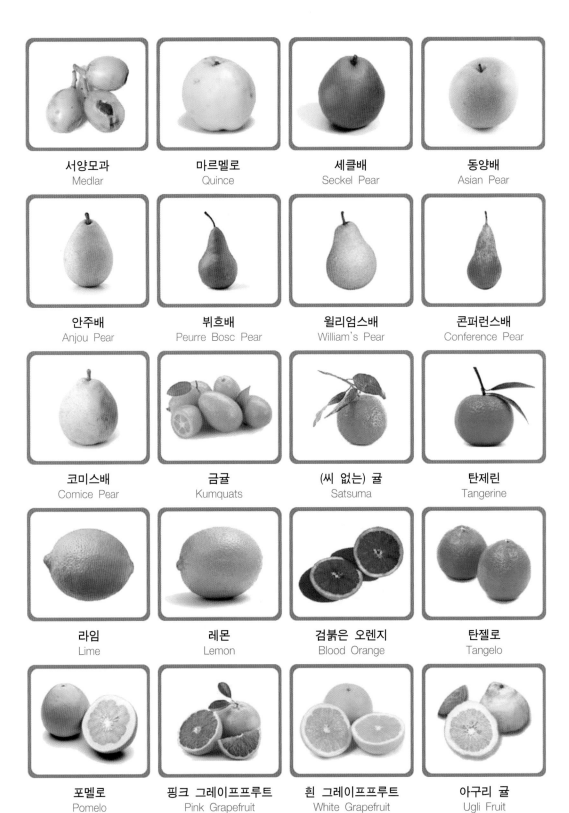

서양모과 Medlar	마르멜로 Quince	세클배 Seckel Pear	동양배 Asian Pear
안주배 Anjou Pear	뷔흐배 Peurre Bosc Pear	윌리엄스배 William's Pear	콘퍼런스배 Conference Pear
코미스배 Comice Pear	금귤 Kumquats	(씨 없는) 귤 Satsuma	탄제린 Tangerine
라임 Lime	레몬 Lemon	검붉은 오렌지 Blood Orange	탄젤로 Tangelo
포멜로 Pomelo	핑크 그레이프프루트 Pink Grapefruit	흰 그레이프프루트 White Grapefruit	아구리 귤 Ugli Fruit

2) 과일명이 쓰이는 주방 실무회화

❶ 소영 씨, 옆 주방 가서 귤 2개만 얻어 오세요.
→ Soyoung, get two tangerines from the next kitchen.

응용 Get a half dozen of eggs from the fridge.

> 참고
> 1. a half dozen : 6개(a dozen이 12개이므로 그것의 절반이라는 뜻으로 쓰임)
> 2. fridge : refrigerator의 짧은 표현. 일반 회화체에서 널리 쓰임

❷ 소영 씨, 금귤은 얇게 썰어서 칩으로 만드세요.
→ Soyoung, slice kumquats thinly and make them as chips.

응용 Slice an onion for me.

❸ 소영 씨, 핑크자몽을 세그먼트(segment)해요.
→ Soyoung, segment a pink grapefruit.

응용 Peel off 10 mangoes.

> 참고
> 세그먼트란 오렌지, 레몬, 자몽 같은 과일(시트러스류)을 점선처럼 조각내는 것을 뜻한다.

❹ 소영 씨, 레몬즙을 약간 짜 넣으세요.
→ Soyoung, squeeze a little bit of lemon juice.

응용 Sprinkle a little bit of salt on the meat.

복숭아
Peach

천도복숭아
Nectarine

살구
Apricot

빙 체리
Bing Cherry

자두
Plum

산딸기
Raspberry

딸기
Strawberry

블랙베리
Blackberry

구스베리
Gooseberry

크랜베리
Cranberry

화이트커런트
White Currant

레드커런트
Red Currant

로간베리
Loganberry

건포도
Raisin

수박
Watermelon

샤랑테멜론
Charentais Melon

참외
Yellow Melon

허니듀멜론
Honeydew Melon

시계꽃 열매
Passion Fruit

칸탈루프
Cantaloupe

3) 과일명이 쓰이는 주방 실무회화

❶ 소영 씨, 복숭아 통조림 몇 개 있어요?

→ Soyoung, how many peach cans do we have?

[응용] How many reservations do we have tonight?

❷ 소영 씨, 이 수박이 맛이 없어요.

→ Soyoung, this watermelon tastes awful.

[응용] This steak tastes terrible.

> 참고
> '맛이 형편없다'라는 표현으로 '~tastes terrible'을 쓴다는 것을 기억하자!

❸ 소영 씨, 건살구를 이용해서 카나페를 만들어요.

→ Soyoung, make canapes with dried apricots.

[응용] Make canapes with eggs.

❹ 소영 씨, 구스베리 창고에 있어요?

→ Soyoung, do we have gooseberry in the stock room?

[응용] Do we have honeydews in the stock room?

❺ 소영 씨, 패션 프루츠는 중식주방에서 쓰나요?

→ Soyoung, are passion fruits used in a Chinese kitchen?

[응용] Are cranberries used in a Chinese kitchen?

석류
Pomegranate

파인애플
Pineapple

망고
Mango

바나나
Banana

구아바
Guava

감
Persimmon

망고스틴
Mangosteen

대추
Jujube

리치
Lychee

무화과
Fig

잣
Pine Nut

헤이즐넛
Hazelnut

아몬드
Almond

땅콩
Peanut

호두
Walnut

밤
Chestnut

캐슈넛
Cashew Nut

피스타치오
Pistachio Nut

마카다미아
Macadamia Nut

피칸
Pecan Nut

4) 과일명이 쓰이는 주방 실무회화

❶ 소영 씨, 바나나가 너무 익었어요.

→ Soyoung, the bananas are too ripe.

[응용] The mangos are too ripe.

❷ 소영 씨, 피스타치오 껍질은 더운물에 불려야 잘 벗겨져요.

→ Soyoung, it's easy to peel off pistachio after soaking them up in water.

[응용] Leave pistachio in water for 30 minutes for easier peeling off.

❸ 소영 씨, 껍질 벗긴 호두를 쓰세요.

→ Soyoung, use the peeled walnuts.

[응용] Use the peeled pistachio nuts.

❹ 소영 씨, 감은 셔벗으로 만들어요.

→ Soyoung, make sherbet with a persimmon.

[응용] Make sherbet with a pineapple.

❺ 소영 씨, 무화과는 껍질을 벗기고 반을 잘라요.

→ Soyoung, peel off the figs and cut them in half.

[응용] Peel off guavas and cut them in half.

2. 야채류

가지 Eggplant	감자 Potato	강낭콩 Kidney Bean	고구마 Sweet Potato
고추 Chili	당근 Carrot	보리 Barley	밀 Wheat
플럼토마토 Plum Tomato	토마토 Tomato	방울토마토 Cherry Tomato	대추방울토마토 Jujube Cherry Tomato
셀러리 Celery	마늘 Garlic	양배추 Cabbage	양파 Onion
연근 Lotus Root	오이 Cucumber	완두콩 Pea	죽순 Bamboo Shoot

1) 야채명이 쓰이는 주방 실무회화

❶ 소영 씨, 감자 껍질 벗길 때 필러(peeler)를 사용해요.
→ Soyoung, use a peeler when you peel off a potato skin.

(응용) Use a spatula to scrape the pan.

❷ 소영 씨, 아스파라거스 몇 개나 있어요?
→ How much asparagus do we have?

(응용) How many heads of cabbages do we have?

❸ 소영 씨, 양배추는 슬라이스 기계로 썰어요.
→ We use a machine to slice cabbages.

(응용) We use a peeler to peel off oranges.

❹ 소영 씨, 셀러리는 렐리시로 좋은 재료예요.
→ Celery is a great ingredient for relish.

(응용) Tomatoes are good for salads.

❺ 소영 씨, 오이는 반 자르고 스쿱을 사용해서 씨를 제거해요.
→ Soyoung, cut the cucumber in half and use a scoop to remove the seeds.

(응용) Peel off the cucumber and slice them diagonally.

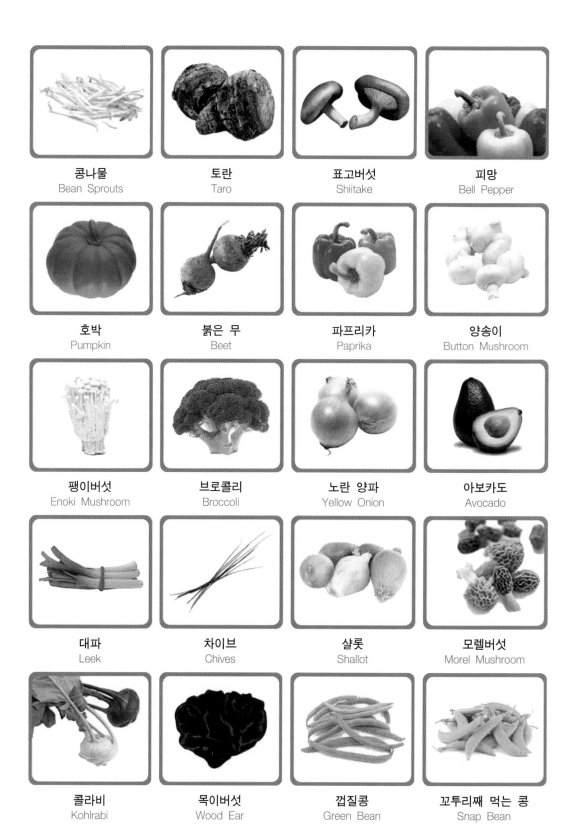

콩나물 Bean Sprouts	**토란** Taro	**표고버섯** Shiitake	**피망** Bell Pepper
호박 Pumpkin	**붉은 무** Beet	**파프리카** Paprika	**양송이** Button Mushroom
팽이버섯 Enoki Mushroom	**브로콜리** Broccoli	**노란 양파** Yellow Onion	**아보카도** Avocado
대파 Leek	**차이브** Chives	**샬롯** Shallot	**모렐버섯** Morel Mushroom
콜라비 Kohlrabi	**목이버섯** Wood Ear	**껍질콩** Green Bean	**꼬투리째 먹는 콩** Snap Bean

2) 야채명이 쓰이는 주방 실무회화

❶ 소영 씨, 아보카도 잘 익었어요?

→ Soyoung, are the avocados ripen enough?

(응용) Are the tomatoes ripen enough?

❷ 소영 씨, 콩나물은 살짝 데쳐주세요.

→ Soyoung, blanch the bean sprouts slightly.

(응용) Saute the vegetables in hot water for a few seconds.

❸ 소영 씨, 양송이버섯은 1/4로 썰어주세요.

→ Soyoung, cut the mushrooms in quarters.

(응용) Cut the pumpkin in cubes.

❹ 소영 씨, 샬롯이 상한 것 같아요.

→ Soyoung, the shallots seem to be gone bad.

(응용) The eggs seem to be gone bad.

❺ 소영 씨, 대파 파란 부위는 버리세요.

→ Soyoung, get rid of the green part of the leek.

(응용) Remove the egg whites.

마
Yam

스파게티호박
Spaghetti Marrow

노란 애호박
Yellow Young Pumpkin

버터호두호박
Butternut Squash

가지
Aubergine

주키니
Zucchini

콜리플라워
Cauliflower

그린올리브
Green Olive

블랙올리브
Black Olive

무
Radish

하리코베르콩
Haricots Verts

화이트 트러플
White Truffle

블랙 트러플
Black Truffle

석이버섯
Dried Cloud Ear

비트루트
Beetroot

셀러리악
Celeriac

파스닙
Parsnip

펜넬
Fennel

아티초크
Artichoke

아스파라거스
Asparagus

3) 야채명이 쓰이는 주방 실무회화

❶ 소영 씨, 토마토를 살짝 삶아서 껍질을 벗기세요.
→ Soyoung, peel off tomato skin after blanching.

응용 Peel off onion skin.

❷ 소영 씨, 비트루트는 흰 도마에서 썰면 물들어서 안돼요.
→ Soyoung, do not cut beet roots on a white cutting board.

응용 Do not use a white cutting board to slice cabbage Kimchi.

❸ 소영 씨, 블랙올리브 다져서 타프나드 만들어요.
→ Soyoung, chop the black olives to make tapenade.

응용 Chop the garlic finely.

❹ 소영 씨, 아티초크 다듬을 시간 있어요?
→ Soyoung, do you have time to prepare artichokes?

응용 Do you have time to garnish the dishes?

❺ 소영 씨, 내일은 셀러리악 수프 만들어야 해요!
→ Soyoung, we need to make celeriac soup tomorrow.

응용 We need to prepare 100 pot pies tomorrow.

Tip

• 셀러리악 •

이 채소는 강한 셀러리와 파슬리의 중간 정도의 맛이 난다. 셀러리의 일종으로, 둥근 뿌리를 얻기 위해 재배한다. 껍질을 벗기면 단단한 질감의 속살이 드러난다. 일반적으로 잎은 버리고 껍질을 벗겨 감자와 함께 갈아 매시로 만들거나 크로켓 같은 요리로 만들 수 있다. 또한 피클로도 만들 수 있다.

3. 곡류

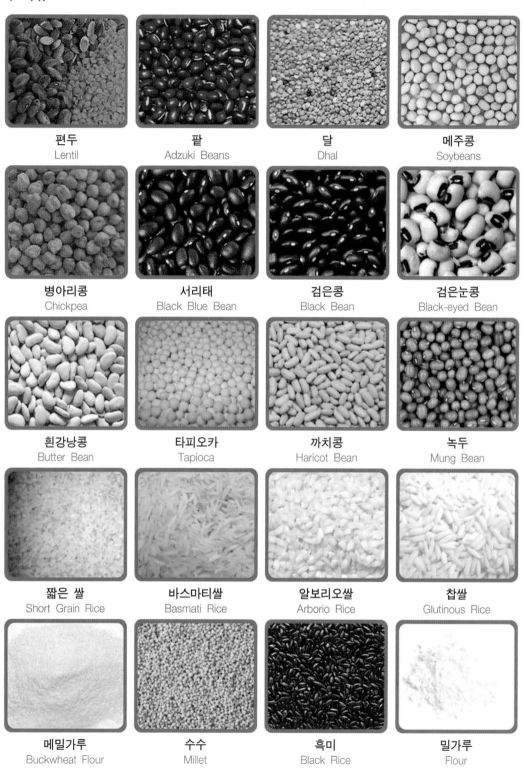

편두 Lentil	**팥** Adzuki Beans	**달** Dhal	**메주콩** Soybeans
병아리콩 Chickpea	**서리태** Black Blue Bean	**검은콩** Black Bean	**검은눈콩** Black-eyed Bean
흰강낭콩 Butter Bean	**타피오카** Tapioca	**까치콩** Haricot Bean	**녹두** Mung Bean
짧은 쌀 Short Grain Rice	**바스마티쌀** Basmati Rice	**알보리오쌀** Arborio Rice	**찹쌀** Glutinous Rice
메밀가루 Buckwheat Flour	**수수** Millet	**흑미** Black Rice	**밀가루** Flour

1) 곡물명이 쓰이는 주방 실무회화

❶ 소영 씨, 밀가루 체에 내렸어요?
→ Soyoung, did you shift the flour?

(응용) Did you clean the cutting board?

❷ 소영 씨, 병아리콩(chick peas) 갈아서 호무스(hommus) 만드세요.
→ Soyoung, grind chick peas and make hommus.

(응용) Grind the garlic and ginger.

❸ 소영 씨, 리조토는 알보리오(쌀의 한 종류)를 사용하세요.
→ Soyoung, use arborio rice to make a risotto dish.

(응용) Use buckwheat flour to make noodles.

❹ 소영 씨, 녹두 좀 갈아줄래요?
→ Soyoung, can you please grind 1 cup of mung beans for me?

(응용) Can you please grind 1 cup of tapioca for me?

❺ 소영 씨, 고기에 춘장소스(black bean sauce) 좀 발라요.
→ Soyoung, apply black bean sauce on the meat.

(응용) Apply sesame seed oil on the meat.

4. 허브류

아루굴라 Arugula	컬리 엔다이브 Curly Endive
청경채 Bok Choy	콜라드그린 Collard Green
라디치오 Radicchio	소렐 Sorrel
근대잎 Swiss Chard Leaf	깻잎 Sesame Leaf
벨기에 엔다이브 Belgium Endive	로메인 상추 Romaine Lettuce
롤로 로소 Lollo Rosso	배추 Chinese Cabbage
크레송 Watercress	레드 엔다이브 Red Endive
양상추 Iceberg Lettuce	머스터드잎 Mustard Leaf
무순 Mustard Cress	래디시 Radish
민들레잎 Red Dandelion	그린 비타민 Green Vitamin

1) 허브명이 쓰이는 주방 실무회화

❶ 소영 씨, 특수야채 들어오면 일단 얼음물에 담가요.
→ Soyoung, when special vegetables arrive, put them in icy water.

(응용) Rinse the vegetables in chilled water.

> 참고
> icy 또는 iced water는 얼음처럼 찬물 혹은 얼음 넣은 찬물을 뜻하고,
> chilled water는 차갑게 식힌 물 또는 냉수를 말한다.

❷ 소영 씨, 라디치오 말라요. 빨리 젖은 천으로 덮어주세요.
→ Soyoung, radicchioes are getting dry. Put them with a damp cloth.

(응용) The meats are getting dry. Cover them up.

❸ 소영 씨, 아루굴라에 흙이 많으니 깨끗이 씻어요.
→ Soyoung, rinse the dirt from the arugulas.

(응용) Rinse the strawberries thoroughly.

❹ 소영 씨, 오늘 크레송 들어온 것 싱싱해요?
→ Soyoung, are the water cresses of today fresh?

(응용) Are the blueberries fresh?

❺ 소영 씨, 청경채 좀 데쳐줄래요?
→ Soyoung, can you blanch the bok choy?

(응용) Can you blanch the asparagus on the table?

Tip

> **• 청경채 •**
>
> 중국이 원산지인 채소로 서늘한 지역에서는 연중 재배가 가능하다. 보통 쌈채소로 인식하고 있지만 순한 맛과 아삭한 질감으로 인해 동남아뿐만 아니라 전 세계적으로 다양한 요리로 활용되고 있다.

5. 스파이스류

계피
Cinnamon

고수
Cilantro

로즈마리
Rosemary

민트
Mint

세이지
Sage

아니스
Anise

와사비
Wasabi

월계수잎
Bay Leaf

정향
Dried Clove Buds

커리
Curry

커민
Cumin

백리향
Thyme

강황
Turmeric

파슬리
Parsley

후추
Black Pepper

마조람
Marjoram

딜
Dill

바질
Basil

사철쑥
Perennial Artemisia

오레가노
Oregano

1) 스파이스명이 쓰이는 주방 실무회화

❶ 소영 씨, 이 도마에는 허브 다지지 말아요!
→ Soyoung, don't chop herbs on this cutting board.
응용 Don't chop garlic on this cutting board.

❷ 소영 씨, 고수는 잎만 다져주세요.
→ Soyoung, chop only the cilantro leaves.
응용 Chop the parsley finely.

❸ 소영 씨, 바질잎 하나도 없어요?
→ Soyoung, we don't have any basil leaves at all?
응용 Do we have any basil leaves?

❹ 소영 씨, 디저트 장식으로 민트잎 꽂아주세요!
→ Soyoung, garnish with mint leaves.
응용 Garnish with herbs.

❺ 소영 씨, 검은 후추 좀 으깨줄래요?
→ Soyoung, can you crush some black pepper?
응용 Can you garnish the dish, please?

마늘
Garlic

주니퍼베리
Juniper Berry

생강
Ginger

바닐라
Vanilla

사프란
Saffron

육두구
Nutmeg

참깨
Sesame Seed

카다멈 씨앗
Cardamom Seeds

캐러웨이씨
Caraway Seeds

파프리카가루
Paprika Powder

할라피뇨 고추
Jalapeno Pepper

레몬그라스
Lemon Grass

카옌페퍼
Cayenne Pepper

올스파이스
Allspice

그린페퍼콘
Green Peppercorn

블랙페퍼콘
Black Peppercorn

화이트페퍼콘
White Peppercorn

핑크색 통후추
Pink Peppercorn

페누그릭 씨
Fenugreek Seed

메이스
Mace

2) 스파이스명이 쓰이는 주방 실무회화

❶ 소영 씨, 드레싱에 식초가 너무 많이 들어갔어요.
→ Soyoung, there's too much vinegar in the dressing.

응용 There's too much wasabi in the sauce.

❷ 소영 씨, 여기에는 파프리카가루를 많이 넣어주세요.
→ Soyoung, put lots of paprika powder in here.

응용 Put lots of olive oil in here.

❸ 소영 씨, 다진 마늘 거의 다 써가네요!
→ Soyoung, we're almost running out of minced garlic.

응용 We're almost running out of minced ginger.

❹ 소영 씨, 오리엔탈 드레싱에 레몬그라스를 더 다져 넣어요.
→ Soyoung, put more chopped lemon grass in the oriental dressing.

응용 Put more of chopped hot pepper in here.

❺ 소영 씨, 할라피뇨 좀 갈아주세요.
→ Soyoung, grind some jalapeno for me.

응용 Grind some black pepper.

6. 어패류

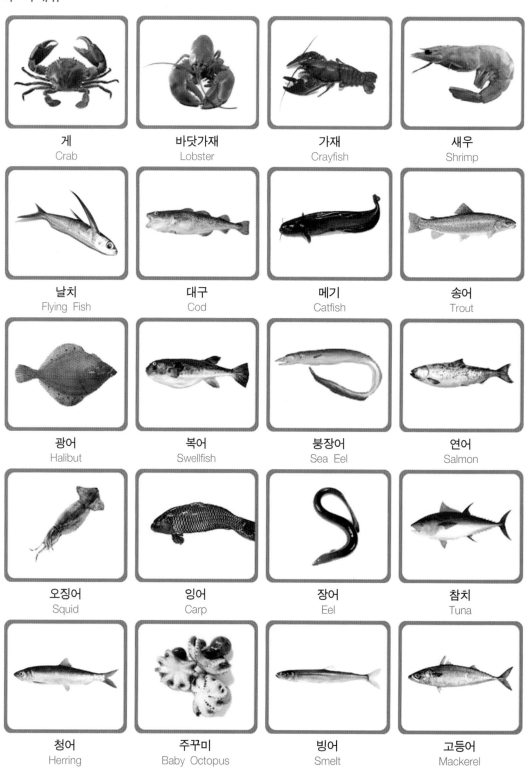

게
Crab

바닷가재
Lobster

가재
Crayfish

새우
Shrimp

날치
Flying Fish

대구
Cod

메기
Catfish

송어
Trout

광어
Halibut

복어
Swellfish

붕장어
Sea Eel

연어
Salmon

오징어
Squid

잉어
Carp

장어
Eel

참치
Tuna

청어
Herring

주꾸미
Baby Octopus

빙어
Smelt

고등어
Mackerel

1) 어패류명이 쓰이는 주방 실무회화

❶ 셰프, 청어 유통기한이 지났는데요?
  → Chef, the expiration date is over for herrings.

  응용 Please check the canned herrings' expiration date.
  * canned herrings : 청어 통조림

❷ 소영 씨, 게 상태가 그리 좋지 않아요.
  → Soyoung, the crabs don't look good.

  응용 The crabs are getting bad.

❸ 소영 씨, 날치알 반은 냉동시켜 주세요.
  → Soyoung, freeze the half of the flying fish roes.

  응용 Keep the flying fish roes chilled.

❹ 소영 씨, 바닷가재 다듬고, 내장은 버리지 마세요.
  → Soyoung, prepare the lobster and do not throw away the giblets.

  응용 Clean the giblets of chickens.

❺ 소영 씨, 광어 뼈를 발라주세요.
  → Soyoung, remove the bones of a halibut.

  응용 Remove the bones of a chicken.

• 유통기한 관련 중요 문장 •

유통기한을 표시하다	define the expiration date
유통기한을 알다	know shelf-life period
유통기한을 넘기다	expires distribution term
유통기한을 위반하다	violate expiration date
유통기한을 알아보다	check out expiration date

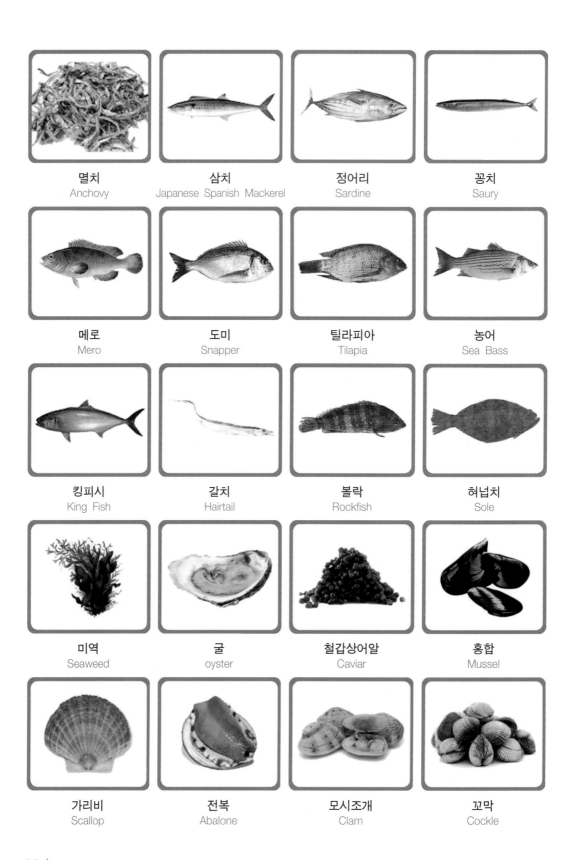

멸치 Anchovy	삼치 Japanese Spanish Mackerel	정어리 Sardine	꽁치 Saury
메로 Mero	도미 Snapper	틸라피아 Tilapia	농어 Sea Bass
킹피시 King Fish	갈치 Hairtail	볼락 Rockfish	혀넙치 Sole
미역 Seaweed	굴 oyster	철갑상어알 Caviar	홍합 Mussel
가리비 Scallop	전복 Abalone	모시조개 Clam	꼬막 Cockle

2) 어패류명이 쓰이는 주방 실무회화

❶ 소영 씨, 도미는 통째로 튀기세요.

→ Soyoung, deep fry the snapper.

(응용) Pan fry the snappers, please.

❷ 소영 씨, 앤초비는 짜니까 조금만 넣어요.

→ Soyoung, put a little bit of anchovy because it's very salty.

(응용) Put a dash of salt.

❸ 소영 씨, 농어 스테이크에 밑간(소금, 후추) 했어요?

→ Soyoung, did you put salt and pepper on a bass?

(응용) Put salt and pepper on a steak.

❹ 소영 씨, 혀넙치는 밀가루를 묻혀 팬에서 구우세요.

→ Soyoung, coat the sole with flour and fry it on the pan.

(응용) Coat snapper with olive oil.

❺ 소영 씨, 갈치비늘 잘 벗겨요.

→ Soyoung, scrape off the scales of a hairtail.

(응용) Scrape off all the dirt from the carrots.

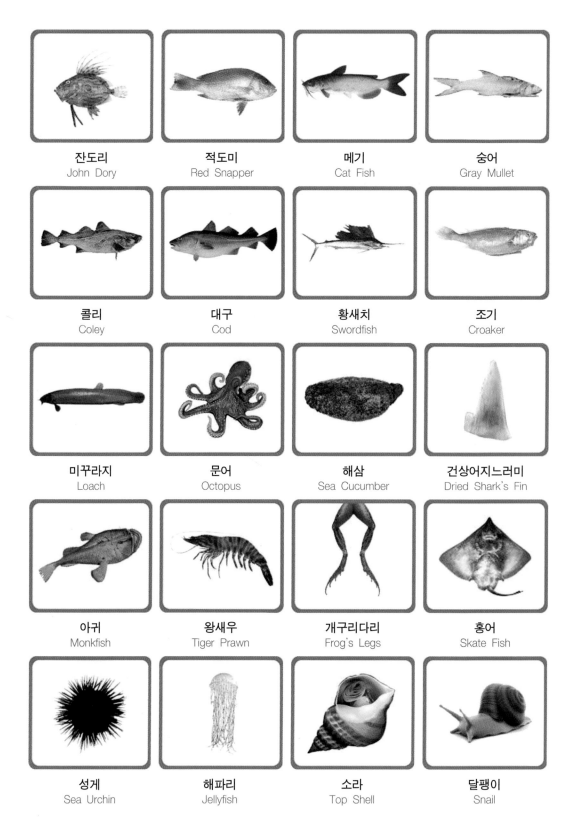

잔도리 John Dory	**적도미** Red Snapper	**메기** Cat Fish	**숭어** Gray Mullet
콜리 Coley	**대구** Cod	**황새치** Swordfish	**조기** Croaker
미꾸라지 Loach	**문어** Octopus	**해삼** Sea Cucumber	**건상어지느러미** Dried Shark's Fin
아귀 Monkfish	**왕새우** Tiger Prawn	**개구리다리** Frog's Legs	**홍어** Skate Fish
성게 Sea Urchin	**해파리** Jellyfish	**소라** Top Shell	**달팽이** Snail

3) 어패류명이 쓰이는 주방 실무회화

❶ 소영 씨, 어제 해파리 몇 킬로 주문 나갔지요?

→ Soyoung, how much jellyfish did we order yesterday?

응용 How much crab did we order?

❷ 소영 씨, 일식주방에서 성게 조금만 빌려오세요.

→ Soyoung, borrow some sea urchin from the Japanese kitchen.

응용 Borrow two cups of soy sauce from the Japanese kitchen.

❸ 소영 씨, 민물가재 손질할 때 손 조심해요.

→ Soyoung, watch out your hands when you clean up yabby.

응용 Be careful when you clean up sea urchin.

❹ 소영 씨, 왕새우는 반드시 쿠르부용(court bouillon)에 삶아야 해요.

→ Soyoung, you should boil the king prawns in court bouillon.

응용 You should use court bouillon to steam the king prawns.

❺ 소영 씨, 달팽이 스튜(snail ragu)에 크림 많이 넣어주세요!

→ Soyoung, put lots of creme in snail ragu.

응용 Put lots of creme in the creme sauce.

❻ 소영 씨, 카나페에는 벨루가 캐비어(beluga caviar)를 사용하세요.

→ Soyoung, use beluga caviar on canapes.

응용 Use goose liver on canapes.

7. 육류, 가금류

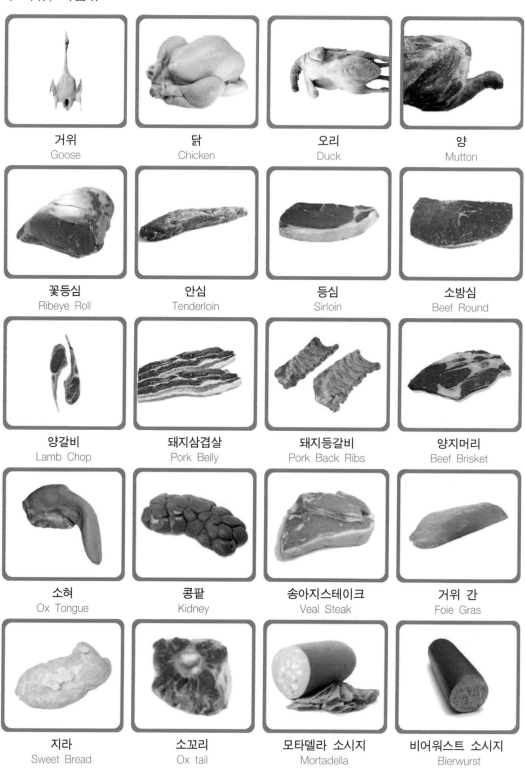

거위
Goose

닭
Chicken

오리
Duck

양
Mutton

꽃등심
Ribeye Roll

안심
Tenderloin

등심
Sirloin

소방심
Beef Round

양갈비
Lamb Chop

돼지삼겹살
Pork Belly

돼지등갈비
Pork Back Ribs

양지머리
Beef Brisket

소혀
Ox Tongue

콩팥
Kidney

송아지스테이크
Veal Steak

거위 간
Foie Gras

지라
Sweet Bread

소꼬리
Ox tail

모타델라 소시지
Mortadella

비어워스트 소시지
Bierwurst

1) 육류, 가금류명이 쓰이는 주방 실무회화

❶ 소영 씨, 양고기에는 다진 허브 많이 넣어요.
  → Soyoung, put a lot of finely chopped herbs in lamb.

  응용 Put 1 teaspoonful of finely chopped garlic.

❷ 소영 씨, 불고기소스에 고기를 재워주세요.
  → Soyoung, marinate the beef with the bulgogi sauce.

  응용 Marinate all the ingredients with the new sauce.

❸ 소영 씨, 양갈비 기름 제거해 주세요.
  → Soyoung, get rid of fat from the lamb ribs.

  응용 Get rid of fat from the chicken.

❹ 셰프, 오늘 들어온 소꼬리에 기름이 너무 많아요!
  → Chef, there's too much fat in the ox tail we have today.

  응용 There's too much fat in the lamb.

❺ 소영 씨, 푸아그라 힘줄 제거해요.
  → Soyoung, remove the stringy parts from the foie gras.

  응용 Remove the fat from the pork.

8. 유제품류

버터
Butter

저지방우유
Low Fat Milk

크림치즈
Cream Cheese

고다치즈
Gouda Cheese

고르곤졸라치즈
Gorgonzola Cheese

그뤼에르치즈
Gruyere Cheese

카망베르치즈
Camembert Cheese

모차렐라치즈
Mozzarella Cheese

브리치즈
Brie Cheese

에멘탈치즈
Emmental Cheese

염소젖치즈
Goat Cheese

체더치즈
Cheddar Cheese

파르메산치즈
Parmesan Cheese

페타치즈
Feta Cheese

스틸턴치즈
Stilton Cheese

마스카르포네치즈
Mascarpone Cheese

론델레치즈
Rondele Cheese

코티지치즈
Cottage Cheese

테트 드 무안치즈
Tete de Moine Cheese

아펜젤러치즈
Appenzeller Cheese

1) 유제품명이 쓰이는 주방 실무회화

❶ 소영 씨, 크림치즈 잘 안 갈리면 우유를 조금 넣어봐요.
→ Soyoung, add a little milk if the cheese doesn't grind well.

> (응용) Add a little wine.

❷ 소영 씨, 쓰다 남은 치즈는 버리지 말고 갈아서 사용해요.
→ Soyoung, don't throw away the left over cheese but use it by grinding it.

> (응용) Don't throw away the left over wine.

❸ 소영 씨, 뷔페에 페타치즈 샐러드 다 떨어졌어요!
→ Soyoung, we're out of peta cheese salad on buffet.

> (응용) We're out of spaghetti on buffet.

❹ 소영 씨, 정제버터(clarified butter)가 다 떨어졌어요.
→ Soyoung, we're out of clarified butter.

> (응용) We're out of raclette cheese.

❺ 소영 씨, 치즈보드에는 프렌치 치즈만 올려요.
→ Soyoung, just put French cheese on a cheese board.

> (응용) Just put canapes and cheese on this plate.

9. 양념류

화이트와인식초
White Wine Vinegar

레드와인식초
Red Wine Vinegar

발사믹식초
Balsamic Vinegar

셰리식초
Sherry Vinegar

타라곤식초
Tarragon Vinegar

쌀식초
Rice Vinegar

사이다식초
Cider Vinegar

맥아식초
Malt Vinegar

샴페인식초
Champagne Vinegar

미국식 머스터드
American Mustard

영국식 머스터드
English Mustard

독일식 머스터드
German Mustard

토마토케첩
Tomato Ketchup

칠리소스
Chili Sauce

생선소스
Fish Sauce

앤초비 페이스트
Anchovy Paste

망고 처트니
Mango Chutney

메이플시럽
Maple Syrup

타바스코
Tabasco

토마토 퓌레
Tomato Puree

1) 양념명이 쓰이는 주방 실무회화

❶ 소영 씨, 드레싱에 식초가 너무 많이 들어갔어요.

→ Soyoung, there's to much vinegar in the dressing.

(응용) Put more vinegar into the dressing.

❷ 소영 씨, 사우전드 아일랜드 드레싱(thousand island dressing)에 타바스코 더 넣으세요

→ Soyoung, put more tabasco sauce into the thousand island dressing.

(응용) Put more herbs into the dressing.

❸ 소영 씨, 아메리칸 머스터드 쓰고 뚜껑을 덮으세요.

→ Soyoung, close the lid after using the American mustard.

(응용) Close the lid of the steamer.

❹ 셰프, 이탈리안 드레싱 만들 때 레드와인 식초 얼마나 들어가요?

→ Chef, how much red wine vinegar do we put to make Italian dressing?

(응용) How much garlic do we put to make Italian dressing?

❺ 셰프, 태국음식에 피시소스를 많이 쓰나요?

→ Chef, do you use a lot of fish sauce in Thai cuisine?

(응용) Do you use a lot of fish sauce in Vietnamese cuisine?

10. 파스타류

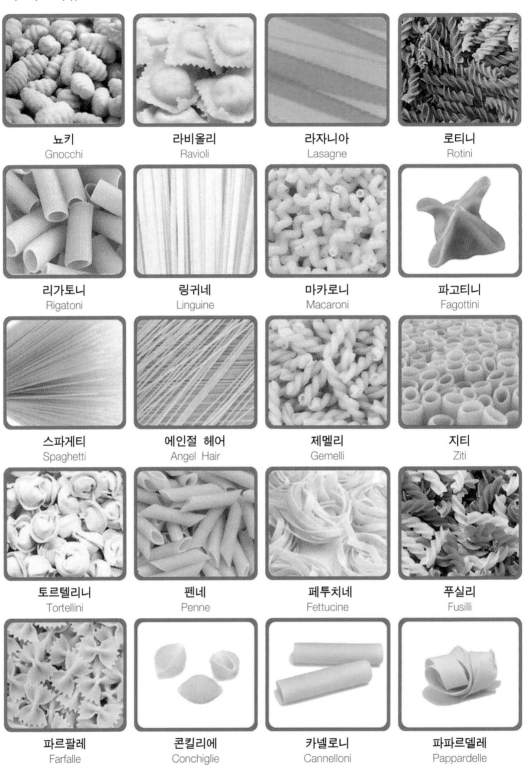

뇨키 Gnocchi	**라비올리** Ravioli	**라자니아** Lasagne	**로티니** Rotini
리가토니 Rigatoni	**링귀네** Linguine	**마카로니** Macaroni	**파고티니** Fagottini
스파게티 Spaghetti	**에인절 헤어** Angel Hair	**제멜리** Gemelli	**지티** Ziti
토르텔리니 Tortellini	**펜네** Penne	**페투치네** Fettucine	**푸실리** Fusilli
파르팔레 Farfalle	**콘킬리에** Conchiglie	**카넬로니** Cannelloni	**파파르델레** Pappardelle

1) 파스타명이 쓰이는 주방 실무회화

❶ 소영 씨, 스파게티 너무 많이 익히지 마세요.
→ Soyoung, do not overcook the spaghetti.

(응용) Boil spaghetti only for 5-6 minutes.

❷ 소영 씨, 라비올리 만들게 달걀노른자 좀 주세요.
→ Soyoung, get some egg yolks to make ravioli.

(응용) Beat egg whites for me.

❸ 소영 씨, 로티니 없으면 푸실리로 대체해요.
→ Soyoung, replace with fusili if you don't have rotini.

(응용) Replace angel hair with spaghetti

❹ 소영 씨, 페투치네 미리 삶아놓지 마세요.
→ Soyoung, don't precook fettucine in advance.

(응용) Do not precook macaroni.

❺ 소영 씨, 라인에 리가토니가 떨어졌네요.
→ Soyoung, we're out of rigatoni in the line.

(응용) We're out of lasagne dough in the line.

11. 알코올성 음료류

김렛 Gimlet	다이키리 Daiquiri	마르가리타 Margarita	맨해튼 Manhattan
미모사 Mimosa	블랙벨벳 Black Velvet	블러디메리 Bloody Mary	진 피즈 Gin Fizz
톰 콜린스 Tom Collins	블랙러시안 Black Russian	코냑 Cognac	브랜디 Brandy
보드카 Vodka	위스키 Whisky	럼 Rum	진 Gin
레드와인 Red Wine	로제와인 Rosé Wine	스파클링와인 Sparkling Wine	화이트와인 White Wine

1) 알코올성 음료명이 쓰이는 주방 실무회화

❶ 소영 씨, 소스에 쓸 와인 있어요?
  → Soyoung, do we have any wine to use for sauce?

  응용 Do we have any wine for sauce today?

❷ 소영 씨, 콩소메에 코냑을 넣었어요?
  → Soyoung, did you put cognac into consome?

  응용 Did you put red wine into the sauce?

❸ 셰프, 브랜디 여기 있어요.
  → Chef, here is a brandy.

  응용 Here it is.

❹ 소영, 레드와인 3병만 따면 될 것 같아요.
  → Chef, we only need 3 bottles of red wine.

  응용 We need 2 bottles of cognac.

❺ 소영, 양배추요리에 써야 하니 레드와인 아껴 써요.
  → Soyoung, save some red wine to use it for lettuce dish.

  응용 Save some cognac for other dishes.

12. 나이프류

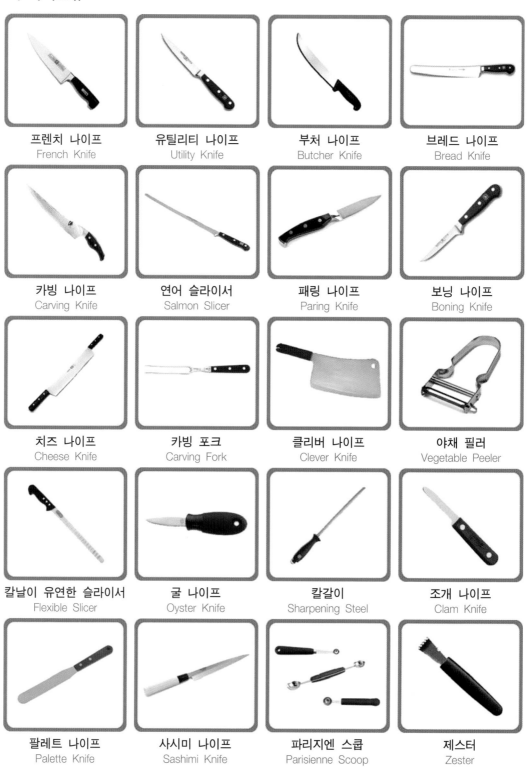

프렌치 나이프
French Knife

유틸리티 나이프
Utility Knife

부처 나이프
Butcher Knife

브레드 나이프
Bread Knife

카빙 나이프
Carving Knife

연어 슬라이서
Salmon Slicer

패링 나이프
Paring Knife

보닝 나이프
Boning Knife

치즈 나이프
Cheese Knife

카빙 포크
Carving Fork

클리버 나이프
Clever Knife

야채 필러
Vegetable Peeler

칼날이 유연한 슬라이서
Flexible Slicer

굴 나이프
Oyster Knife

칼갈이
Sharpening Steel

조개 나이프
Clam Knife

팔레트 나이프
Palette Knife

사시미 나이프
Sashimi Knife

파리지엔 스쿱
Parisienne Scoop

제스터
Zester

1) 나이프명이 쓰이는 주방 실무회화

❶ 소영 씨, 연어 슬라이서(salmon slicer) 못 봤어요?

→ Soyoung, have you seen a salmon slicer?

(응용) Have you seen a carving knife?

❷ 소영 씨, 패링 나이프는 유니폼 주머니에 항상 넣고 다녀요.

→ Soyoung, keep a paring knife in the pocket of your uniform.

(응용) Keep a bone picker in your pocket.

❸ 소영 씨, 칼 쓰고 항상 제자리에 놓으세요.

→ Soyoung, keep the knife in place after using it.

(응용) Keep the knives all in place.

❹ 소영 씨, 출장에 카빙 스테이션 있으니 카빙 나이프 잊지 마요.

→ Soyoung, don't forget to bring a carving knife for outside catering.

(응용) Check all the knives for outside catering.

❺ 소영 씨, 프렌치 나이프는 매일 갈아주세요.

→ Soyoung, sharpen a French knife everyday.

(응용) Sharpen all the knives everyday.

13. 조리기구류

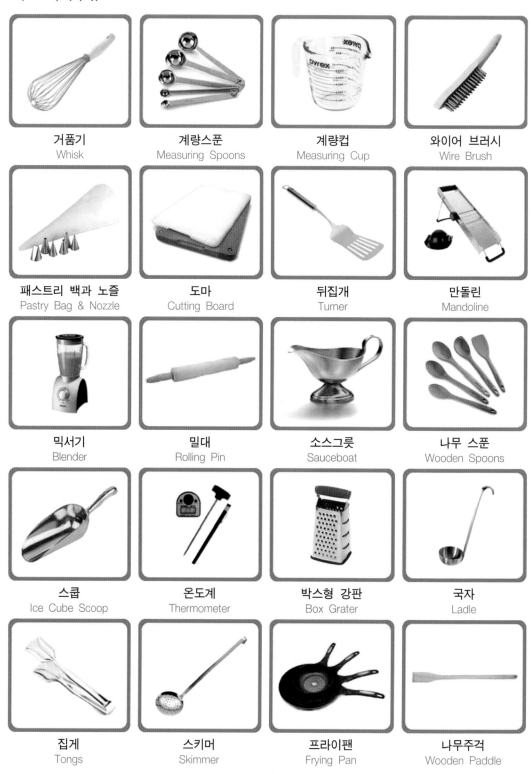

거품기 Whisk	**계량스푼** Measuring Spoons	**계량컵** Measuring Cup	**와이어 브러시** Wire Brush
패스트리 백과 노즐 Pastry Bag & Nozzle	**도마** Cutting Board	**뒤집개** Turner	**만돌린** Mandoline
믹서기 Blender	**밀대** Rolling Pin	**소스그릇** Sauceboat	**나무 스푼** Wooden Spoons
스쿱 Ice Cube Scoop	**온도계** Thermometer	**박스형 강판** Box Grater	**국자** Ladle
집게 Tongs	**스키머** Skimmer	**프라이팬** Frying Pan	**나무주걱** Wooden Paddle

1) 조리기구명이 쓰이는 주방 실무회화

❶ 소영 씨, 도마는 소독기에 넣어주세요.
→ Soyoung, put the cutting board into the sterilizer.
(응용) Sterilize all the cutting boards in a sterilizer.

❷ 소영 씨, 만돌린 좀 닦아줄래요?
→ Soyoung, clean up the mandoline.
(응용) Clean up the ladle.

❸ 소영 씨, 쓰레기통에 이것 좀 버려주세요.
→ Soyoung, throw away this into the trash bin.
(응용) Throw away all the leftovers.

❹ 소영 씨, 소스보트에 소스 좀 담아주세요.
→ Soyoung, put the sauce in a sauceboat.
(응용) Put the sauce in this bowl.

❺ 소영 씨, 집게 좀 빨리 닦아주세요.
→ Soyoung, wipe off the tongs quickly.
(응용) Clean up the tongs quickly.

믹싱 볼
Mixing Bowl

소창
Cheese Cloth

물주전자
Water Kettle

마늘 으깨기
Garlic Press

테린 몰드
Terrine Mold

체
Drum Sieve

가위
Kitchen Scissors

푸드 밀
Food Mill

치즈 스크레이퍼
Cheese Scraper

버터 스크레이퍼
Butter Scraper

사과씨 제거기
Apple Corer

생선가시 제거기
Fish Bone Picker

육류용 망치
Meat Tenderizer

캔 오프너
Can Opener

조리용 바늘
Trussing Needle

페퍼밀
Pepper Mill

달걀 슬라이서
Egg Slicer

고운 소스체
Fine Chinois

굵은 체
China Cap

콜랜더
Colander

2) 조리기구명이 쓰이는 주방 실무회화

❶ 소영 씨, 족집게로 훈제 연어가시 좀 뽑아주세요.
→ Soyoung, pick out the fish bone of the smoked salmon with a fish bone picker.

응용 Be careful with fish bones.

❷ 소영 씨, 미트소는 위험하니까 손대지 말아요.
→ Soyoung, do not touch the meat saw because it's dangerous.

응용 Be careful with the meat saw.

❸ 소영 씨, 제스터(zester) 좀 찾아줄래요?
→ Soyoung, can you find a zester for me?

응용 Can you find a can opener for me?

❹ 소영 씨, 삶은 달걀은 에그 슬라이서로 잘라주세요.
→ Soyoung, slice the boiled eggs with an egg slicer.

응용 Slice the zucchini with a food processor.

❺ 소영 씨, 이것은 캔 오프너로 따야 돼요.
→ Soyoung, you should open this with a can opener.

응용 You should try to open with a knife. Be careful.

14. 주방기기류

슬라이서
Slicer

컨벡션 오븐
Convection Oven

미트 그라인더
Meat Grinder

뱅마리
Bain Marie

토스터기
Toaster

브로일러
Broiler

베지터블 커터
Vegetable Cutter

푸드 블렌더
Food Blender

육절기
Meat Saw

샐러맨더
Salamander

딥 프라이어
Deep Fryer

푸드 워머
Food Warmer

틸팅 스킬릿
Tilting Skillet

그릴
Grill

발효기
Proofer Box

아이스머신
Ice Machine

스팀 케틀
Steam Kettle

시트팬
Sheet Pan

호텔팬
Hotel Pan

보온그릇
Chafing Dish

1) 주방기기명이 쓰이는 주방 실무회화

❶ 소영 씨, 컨벡션 오븐에 등심을 넣어주세요.
  → Soyoung, put the sirloin into the convection oven.

  응용 Put the lamb into the convection oven.

❷ 소영 씨, 닭 다리살은 반죽에 버무려서 기름에 튀겨요.
  → Soyoung, coat the chicken legs into the batter and fry them.

  응용 Coat chicken legs with olive oil.

❸ 소영 씨, 이거 치즈 뿌려서 샐러맨더에 넣어요.
  → Soyoung, sprinkle cheese on this and put it in salamander.

  응용 Sprinkle salt and pepper on this.

❹ 소영 씨, 포스미트(forcemeat)는 푸드 초퍼에 가는 것이 좋아요.
  → Soyoung, it's better to use a food chopper (or processor) to forcemeat.

  응용 It's better to use a food processor to mince a large of quantity of garlic.

❺ 소영 씨, 기물관리부에서 시트팬 30장만 가져다주세요.
  → Soyoung, get 30 sheet pans from the storage room.

  응용 Get 20 sauce pans from the storage room.

Chapter 2

각국의 대표음식과 레시피 독해

Beef Bourguignon
(Serving 2~3)

Ingredients

1 tablespoon good olive oil

8 ounces dry cured center cut applewood smoked bacon, diced

2½ pounds chuck beef cut into 1-inch cubes

Kosher salt

Freshly ground black pepper

1 pound carrots, sliced diagonally into 1-inch chunks

2 yellow onions, sliced

2 teaspoons chopped garlic (2 cloves)

1/2 cup cognac

1 (750ml) bottle good dry red wine such as Cote du Rhone or Pinot Noir

1 can (2 cups) beef broth

1 tablespoon tomato paste

1 teaspoon fresh thyme leaves (1/2 teaspoon dried)

4 tablespoons unsalted butter at room temperature, divided

3 tablespoons all-purpose flour

1 pound frozen whole onions

1 pound fresh mushrooms stems discarded, caps thickly sliced

1 pound=453.6g

1 oz   =28.35g

For serving

- Country bread or Sour Dough, toasted or grilled and rubbed with garlic clove
- 1/2 cup chopped fresh parsley, optional

 **Directions**

❶ Preheat the oven to 250°F.

❷ Heat the olive oil in a large Dutch oven. Add the bacon and cook over medium heat for 10 minutes, stirring occasionally, until the bacon is lightly browned. Remove the bacon with a slotted spoon to a large plate.

❸ Dry the beef cubes with paper towels and then sprinkle them with salt and pepper. In batches in single layers, sear the beef in the hot oil for 3 to 5 minutes, turning to brown on all sides. Remove the seared cubes to the plate with the bacon and continue searing until all the beef is browned. Set aside.

❹ Toss the carrots, and onions, 1 tablespoon of salt and 2 teaspoons of pepper in the fat in the pan and cook for 10 to 15 minutes, stirring occasionally, until the onions are lightly browned. Add the garlic and cook for 1 more minute. Add the Cognac, stand back, and ignite with a match to burn off the alcohol. Put the meat and bacon back into the pot with the juices. Add the bottle of wine plus enough beef broth to almost cover the meat. Add the tomato paste and thyme. Bring to a simmer, cover the pot with a tight-fitting lid and place it in the oven for about 1¼ hours or until the meat and vegetables are very tender when pierced with a fork.

❺ Combine 2 tablespoons of butter and the flour with a fork and stir into the stew. Add the frozen onions. Saute the mushrooms in 2 tablespoons of butter for 10 minutes until lightly browned and then add to the stew. Bring the stew to a boil on top of the stove, then lower the heat and simmer for 15 minutes. Season to taste.

❻ To serve, toast the bread in the toaster or oven. Rub each slice on 1 side with a cut clove of garlic. For each serving, spoon the stew over a slice of bread and sprinkle with parsley.

Vocabulary

1.	chuck beef	소 목살
2.	kosher salt	요오드와 같은 첨가물을 넣지 않은 거친 소금
3.	diagonally	대각선으로(어슷썰기)
4.	chopped	잘게 다진
5.	cognac	프랑스의 중부 코냑에서 생산되는 포도주를 원료로 한 브랜디
6.	broth	육수
7.	all-purpose	다목적의
8.	Dutch oven	철제 냄비
9.	slotted spoon	일자형 숟가락(구멍이 뚫려 있는 큰 스푼)
10.	sprinkle	뿌리다
11.	sear	(불에) 그슬리다
12.	ignite	불을 붙이다
13.	tight-fitting	빡빡한
14.	pierced	찌르다
15.	tomato paste	토마토 페이스트(*페이스트는 고추장 정도의 끈기를 가진 상태)

 ## 재료

올리브오일 1테이블스푼
애플우드 나무로 훈제한 사각 베이컨 8온스
1인치 크기로 깍둑썰기한 소 목살 2½파운드
코셔솔트(요오드와 같은 첨가물을 넣지 않은 거친 소금)
신선한 생후추
어슷썰기한 당근 1파운드
자른 노란 양파 2개
다진 마늘 2티스푼
코냑 1/2컵
레드와인 750ml (Cote du Rhone이나 Pinot Noir 같은 드라이 레드와인)
고기 육수 1캔
토마토 페이스트 1테이블스푼
타임잎 1티스푼
실온에 있는 소금 간 안된(=무염) 버터 4티스푼
다목적 밀가루 3테이블스푼
냉동 통양파 1파운드
두껍게 자른 줄기 제거된 버섯 1파운드

장식 재료

- 마늘을 발라서 토스팅하거나 그릴에 구운 시골빵 또는 사워 도우
- 다진 파슬리 1/2컵(선택사항)

🥣 조리법

① 오븐은 250°F로 예열한다.

② 철제 냄비에 올리브 오일을 넣고 예열한다. 베이컨을 넣고 중간불에서 10분 정도 굽는다. 베이컨은 갈색빛이 돌 때까지 가끔 저어준다. 일자형 숟가락(slotted spoon)으로 베이컨을 접시에 옮겨 담는다.

③ 고기를 겹치지 않게 적정량을 사각썰기하여 키친타월로 물기를 제거한 후 소금과 후추를 살짝 뿌려준다. 각각 묶음으로 나눈 후, 3분에서 5분 정도 고기의 표면을 갈색이 돌도록 뜨거운 기름에 그을린다. 그리고 베이컨과 같이 접시에 옮겨 담는다.

④ 소금 1티스푼, 후추 2티스푼, 당근과 양파를 넓은 팬에 넣고 가끔 저어주며 양파가 갈색이 되도록 10분에서 15분 정도 조리한다. 마늘을 넣고 1분 더 조리한다. 코냑을 넣고 조금 떨어져 불을 붙여서 알코올성분을 날아가게 한다. 고기와 베이컨을 육즙과 함께 냄비에 넣는다. 고기가 잠길 정도로 육수와 와인 1병을 넣는다. 토마토 페이스트와 타임잎을 넣고 끓인다. 딱 맞는 뚜껑을 덮고 오븐에서 1¼시간 동안 굽거나 고기와 채소를 포크로 찔렀을 때 부드럽게 들어갈 정도로 굽는다.

⑤ 버터 2테이블스푼과 밀가루를 포크로 섞어주고 스튜에 넣어 저어준다. 언 양파를 넣는다. 버섯을 버터 2테이블스푼을 넣고 10분간 갈색빛이 돌도록 재빨리 볶아서 스튜에 넣는다. 스튜를 스토브 위에 올리고 낮은 불에서 15분간 끓인다. 양념을 한다.

⑥ 빵을 토스트하거나 오븐에 굽는다. 한쪽에 갈아놓은 마늘을 바른다. 빵과 스튜에 파슬리를 살짝 뿌려준다.

Cheese Blintzes
(Serving 2~3)

Ingredients

[Blintzes]

- 4 ea large beaten eggs
- 1/2 cup water
- 1/2 cup milk
- 1/2 teaspoon salt
- 1 cup all-purpose flour

[Filling]

- 1 pound dry curd or farmers cheese or ricotta
- 1 tablespoon melted butter
- 1 ea large egg yolk
- 2 teaspoons vanilla
- 1/4 cup sugar or more to taste

Directions

① To make the blintzes, beat together all the blintz ingredients and let the batter rest for at least a half hour. Heat a small skillet (about 7 inches) and add a pat of butter. Pour about 1/4 cup batter into the pan and swirl it around, pouring off excess. Don't let it brown. Flip and cook the other side for a few seconds. Then turn blintz out onto a towel. Repeat with remaining batter and pats of butter.

❷ To make the filling, mix together all the filling ingredients in a large bowl.

❸ To assemble, place 1 blintz on a work surface and place 1 tablespoon on top. Fold envelope style and roll up. Continue with remaining blintzes and filling.

❹ Fry filled blintzes in butter until golden brown. Serve with sour cream and / or fruit toppings.

Vocabulary

1.	filling	(파이 등 음식의) 소
2.	curd cheese	커드치즈(부드러운 치즈의 일종)
3.	farmer cheese	파머치즈(전유 또는 일부 탈지한 고형 치즈)
4.	ricotta cheese	리코타(이탈리아산 치즈의 일종)
5.	egg yolk	계란노른자
6.	skillet	스튜용 냄비
7.	swirl	빙빙 젓다.
8.	beaten	(계란 따위를) 터뜨린

 재료

[블린츠]
- 깬 달걀 4개
- 물 1/2컵
- 우유 1/2컵
- 소금 1/2티스푼
- 다목적 밀가루 1컵

[소]
- 커드치즈 또는 파머치즈 또는 리코타치즈 1파운드
- 녹인 버터 1티스푼

- 계란노른자 1개
- 바닐라 2티스푼
- 설탕 1/4컵 또는 더 많이

🥄 만드는 법

① 블린츠를 만들기 위해서 위의 블린츠 재료를 모두 섞는다. 그리고 그 반죽을 적어도 30분 정도 놔둔다. 7인치 정도 되는 작은 스튜용 냄비를 예열하고 한 덩어리의 버터를 넣는다. 그 반죽의 1/4컵을 넣고 저어준다. 여분의 버터는 따라내 버린다. 갈색이 (탈 때까지 두면) 절대 안되고 약간만 익히고, 반대 면도 똑같이 요리한다. 그리고 블린츠를 키친타월 위에 놓는다. 나머지를 똑같이 조리한다.

② 소를 만들기 위해서 모든 소의 재료를 큰 그릇에 섞는다.

③ 블린츠 위에 1테이블스푼의 소를 올리고 봉투모양으로 곱게 만다.

④ 완성된 블린츠를 버터에 금색(황갈색)이 돌도록 튀긴다. 사워크림(Sour Creme) 또는 과일과 함께 장식하면 된다.

Clam Chowder Soup
(Serving 3~4)

Ingredients

3 (6.5 ounce) cans minced clams

1 cup minced onion

1 cup diced celery

2 cups cubed potatoes

1 cup diced carrots

3/4 cup butter

3/4 cup all-purpose flour

1 quart half-and-half cream

2 tablespoons red wine vinegar

1½ teaspoons salt

To taste ground black pepper

Directions

❶ Drain juice from clams into a large skillet over the onions, celery, potatoes and carrots. Add water to cover, and cook over medium heat until tender.

❷ Meanwhile, in a large, heavy saucepan, melt the butter over medium heat. Whisk in flour until smooth. Whisk in cream and stir constantly until thick and smooth. Stir in vegetables and clam juice. Heat through, but do not boil.

❸ Stir in clams just before serving. If they cook too much they get tough. When clams are heated through, stir in vinegar, and season with salt and pepper.

Vocabulary

1.	half-and-half cream	하프앤하프 크림(우유와 생크림을 반반씩 섞어서 만든 크림)
2.	vinegar	식초
3.	drain	물기를 빼다
4.	tough	질긴/딱한
5.	tender	부드러운/연한
6.	constantly	계속해서
7.	thick	걸쭉한/뻑뻑한

 재료

다진 조개 3캔
다진 양파 1컵
깍둑썰기한 셀러리 1컵
네모로 썬 감자 2컵
깍둑썰기한 당근 1컵
버터 3/4컵
다목적 밀가루 3/4컵
하프앤하프 크림 1quart
레드와인식초 2티스푼
소금 1½티스푼
생후추 약간

🥣 만드는 법

❶ 물기 뺀 조개를 양파, 셀러리, 감자, 당근과 함께 냄비에 넣는다. 물을 잠길 정도로 넣고 중간불로 부드러워질 때까지 조리한다.

❷ 그동안 큰 소스팬에 버터를 중불에 녹인다. 밀가루를 넣고 부드러워질 때까지 젓는다. 크림을 넣고 걸쭉하고 부드러워질 때까지 계속해서 젓는다. 야채와 조갯물을 넣고 저어서 끓지 않을 정도로 익힌다. 데우기는 하되 끓이면 안된다.

❸ 조개는 음식을 내놓기 전에 넣는다. 너무 많이 끓이면 조개가 딱딱해지기 때문이다. 조개가 잘 데워진 상태가 되면 식초를 넣고 저은 후에 소금, 후추로 양념한다.

Croque Monsieur
(Serving 4)

Ingredients

2 Tbsp butter

2 Tbsp flour

1½ cups milk

A pinch each of salt, freshly ground pepper, nutmeg, or more to taste

6 ounces Gruyere cheese, grated (about 1½ cups grated)

1/4 cup grated Parmesan cheese (packed)

8 slices of French or Italian loaf bread

12 ounces ham, sliced

To taste Dijon mustard

Directions

❶ Preheat oven to 400°F/200°C.

❷ Make the bechamel sauce. Melt butter in a small saucepan on medium/low heat until it just starts to bubble. Add the flour and cook, stirring until smooth, about 2 minutes. Slowly add the milk, whisking continuously, cooking until thick. Remove from heat. Add the salt, pepper, and nutmeg. Stir in the Parmesan and 1/4 cup of the grated Gruyere. Set aside.

❸ Lay out the bread slices on a baking sheet and toast them in the oven, a few minutes each side, until lightly toasted. For extra flavor you can spread some butter on the bread slices before you toast them if you want.

❹ Lightly brush half of the toasted slices with mustard. Add the ham slices and about 1 cup of the remaining Gruyere cheese. Top with the other toasted bread slices.

❺ Spoon on the bechamel sauce to the tops of the sandwiches. Sprinkle with the remaining Gruyere cheese. Place on a broiling pan. Bake in the oven for 5 minutes, then turn on the broiler and broil for an additional 3 to 5 minutes, until the cheese topping is bubbly and lightly browned.

Tip

If you top this sandwich with a fried egg it becomes a Croque Madame.

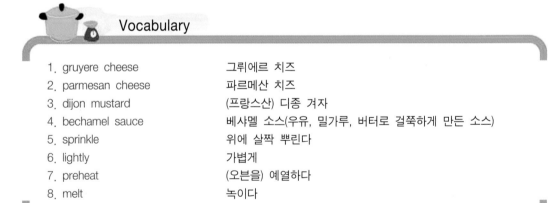

Vocabulary

1.	gruyere cheese	그뤼에르 치즈
2.	parmesan cheese	파르메산 치즈
3.	dijon mustard	(프랑스산) 디종 겨자
4.	bechamel sauce	베샤멜 소스(우유, 밀가루, 버터로 걸쭉하게 만든 소스)
5.	sprinkle	위에 살짝 뿌린다
6.	lightly	가볍게
7.	preheat	(오븐을) 예열하다
8.	melt	녹이다

 재료

버터 2테이블스푼
밀가루 2테이블스푼

우유 1½컵
소금, 생후추, 너트메그
그뤼에르 치즈 6온스
갈아 놓은 파르메산 치즈 1/4컵
프랑스나 이탈리아 빵 8조각
슬라이스된 햄 12온스
디종 겨자 약간

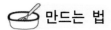 만드는 법

❶ 오븐을 $400°F/200°C$로 예열한다.

❷ 베샤멜 소스를 만든다. 버터를 소스팬에 넣고 중간불/약한 불에 거품이 나기 시작할 때까지 녹인다. 밀가루를 넣고 조리한다. 부드러워질 때까지 2분 정도 젓는다. 우유를 천천히 첨가하고 걸쭉해질 때까지 계속 젓는다. 불을 끄고 소금, 후추, 너트메그를 넣는다. 파르메산 치즈와 $¼\,cup$의 그뤼에르 치즈 섞은 것을 넣고 섞어준다. 옆에다 놓는다.

❸ 베이킹 시트를 깔고 그 위에 자른 빵을 올리고 오븐에 넣어서 양쪽 면을 굽는다. 풍미를 더하기 위해 버터를 빵에 더 바를 수도 있다.

❹ 절반의 구워놓은 빵조각에 디종 머스터드를 살짝 바른다. 햄슬라이스와 약 1컵의 남겨둔 그뤼에르 치즈를 넣는다. 다른 구운 빵을 올린다.

❺ 베샤멜 소스를 샌드위치 위에 숟가락으로 올린다. 그 위에 남겨놓은 그뤼에르 치즈를 뿌린다. 한번 더 올린다. 오븐에 넣고 5분 정도 더 굽는다. 그리고 브로일러를 켜고 치즈토핑에 거품이 나거나 갈색이 날 때까지 추가로 3분에서 5분 동안 브로일러에서 구워낸다.

Tip

이 샌드위치 위에 계란 프라이를 올리면 '크로크 마담'이 된다.

Fish and chips
(Serving 4)

■ Ingredients

beef dripping or oil for deep frying

For the fish

4x175g/6oz thick cod or haddock fillets

225g/8oz self-raising flour

salt and freshly ground black pepper

300ml/10fl oz fridge-cold lager

For the chips

6-8 large floury potatoes

Directions

❶ Preheat the oven to 300°F/150°C and preheat the dripping or oil to 250°F / 120°C.

❷ For the chips, peel the potatoes and cut into whatever size you prefer. Wash well in cold water, drain and pat dry with a clean tea towel. Put the potatoes into the fryer and allow them to fry gently for about 8-10 minutes, until they are soft but still pale. Check they're cooked by piercing with a small, sharp knife. Lift out of the pan and leave to cool slightly on greaseproof paper.

❸ Increase the heat of the fryer to 350°F/180°C.

❹ Season the fish and dust lightly with flour; this enables the batter to stick to the fish.

❺ To make the batter, sift the flour and a pinch of salt into a large bowl and whisk in the lager to give a thick batter, adding a little extra beer if it seems over-thick. It should be the consistency of very thick double cream and should coat the back of a wooden spoon. Season with salt and thickly coat 2 of the fillets with the batter. Carefully place in the hot fat and cook for 8-10 minutes until golden and crispy. Remove from the pan, drain and sit on a baking sheet lined with greaseproof paper, then keep warm in the oven while you cook the remaining 2 fillets in the same way.

❻ Once the fish is cooked, return the chips to the fryer and cook for 2-3 minutes or until golden and crispy. Shake off any excess fat and season with salt before serving with the crispy fish. If liked, you can serve with tinned mushy peas and bread and butter, for the authentic experience!

Vocabulary

1.	flavour / flavor	맛
2.	cod	대구(생선)
3.	haddock	해덕(대구와 비슷하나 그보다 작은 바다 고기)
4.	fillet	포를 뜬 생선 살코기
5.	self-raising flour	베이킹파우더가 든 밀가루
6.	lager	라거(보통 거품이 많이 나는 연한 색의 맥주)
7.	floury	밀가루가 뒤덮인
8.	maris piper	마리스파이퍼(감자의 일종)
9.	king edward	킹 에드워드(감자의 일종)
10.	greaseproof	기름이 안 배는
11.	batter	반죽
12.	sift	체로 치다
13.	tinned	통조림으로 된
14.	mushy peas	삶아 으깬 완두콩
15.	slightly	약간

재료

튀기기 위한 쇠고기 기름 또는 기름

생선튀김 재료
대구나 해덕의 살코기 4x175g/6oz
베이킹파우더가 든 밀가루 225g/8oz
소금과 생후추(방금 간 검은 후추)
차가운 라거맥주 300ml/10fl oz

감자칩 재료
전분함량이 높은 마리스파이퍼 감자 또는 킹 에드워드 감자 6-8개

만드는 법

① 오븐을 300˚F/150˚C로 예열하고 기름을 250˚F/120˚C로 예열한다.

② 칩을 만들기 위해 감자 껍질을 벗기고 감자를 원하는 크기로 잘라둔다. 찬물에 씻은 후 수건으로 물기를 뺀다. 감자를 기름에 넣어 8분에서 10분 정도 조심해서 감자를 튀긴다. 포크로 살짝 찔러서 조리상태를 확인한다. 조리가 다 되면 몇 분간 식힌 후 기름이 안 배는 종이에 옮겨 담는다.

③ 기름을 350˚F/180˚C로 불을 올린다.

④ 생선에 양념을 하고 반죽을 더 잘 묻게 하기 위해 밀가루를 살짝 묻혀준다.

⑤ 반죽을 만들기 위해 밀가루와 소금을 큰 그릇에 받치고 체에 쳐준다. 걸쭉한 반죽을 만들기 위해 라거를 넣고 저어준다. 만약 너무 걸쭉해 보이면 여분의 라거를 추가 하면서 저어준다. 반죽은 매우 걸쭉한 더블크림의 농도가 돼야 하고 나무스푼 뒷면이 덮여야 한다. 소금으로 양념을 하고 반죽을 생선살에 덮는다. 조심스럽게 뜨거운 기름에 옮겨서 8분에서 10분 정도 금색을 띠도록 바삭하게 튀긴다. 기름이 배지 않는 종이 위에 옮겨 담고, 다른 생선살을 요리하는 동안 다 된 요리는 오븐에서 따뜻하게 보관한다.

⑥ 생선요리가 다 되면 감자를 바삭하게 2분에서 3분 정도 한 번 더 튀긴다. 털어서 여분의 기름을 빼고, 내놓기 전에 소금 간을 한다. 삶아 으깬 완두콩통조림, 빵 그리고 버터와 함께 내면 더욱 좋다.

Kung Pao Chicken
(Serving 2-3)

Ingredients

- 1 pound skinless, boneless chicken breast halves
- 2 tablespoons white wine
- 2 tablespoons soy sauce
- 2 tablespoons sesame oil, divided
- 2 tablespoons cornstarch, dissolved in 2 tablespoons water
- 1 ounce hot chile paste
- 1 teaspoon distilled white vinegar
- 2 teaspoons brown sugar
- 4 green onions, chopped
- 1 tablespoon chopped garlic
- 1 (8 ounce) can water chestnuts
- 4 ounces chopped peanuts

Directions

① To Make Marinade : Combine 1 tablespoon wine, 1 tablespoon soy sauce, 1 tablespoon oil and 1 tablespoon cornstarch/water mixture and mix together. Place chicken pieces in a glass dish or bowl and add marinade. Toss to coat. Cover dish and place in refrigerator for about 30 minutes.

❷ To Make Sauce : In a small bowl combine 1 tablespoon wine, 1 tablespoon soy sauce, 1 tablespoon oil, 1 tablespoon cornstarch / water mixture, chili paste, vinegar and sugar. Mix together and add green onion, garlic, water chestnuts and peanuts. In a medium skillet, heat sauce slowly until aromatic.

❸ Meanwhile, remove chicken from marinade and saute in a large skillet until meat is white and juices run clear. When sauce is aromatic, add sauteed chicken to it and let simmer together until sauce thickens.

Vocabulary

1.	skinless	껍질 벗긴
2.	boneless	뼈가 없는
3.	breast	가슴살
4.	cornstarch	옥수수전분
5.	water chestnut	물밤
6.	marinade	(고기, 생선 등을 재는) 양념장
7.	aromatic	향이 좋은
8.	simmer	약한 불에 천천히 조리한다

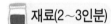 **재료(2~3인분)**

껍질과 뼈가 없는 한입 크기로 자른 닭 가슴살 1파운드
화이트 와인 2테이블스푼
간장소스 2테이블스푼
참기름 2테이블스푼
물 2테이블스푼에 녹인 옥수수전분 2테이블스푼
매운 칠리 페이스트 1온스
증류한 화이트식초 1티스푼
갈색 설탕 2티스푼
다져 썬 파 4개
다져 갈아놓은 마늘 1테이블스푼
밤 통조림 1(8온스)캔
다져 으깬 땅콩 4온스

만드는 법

만드는 법

❶ 양념장 : 와인 1테이블스푼, 간장소스 1테이블스푼, 오일 1테이블스푼, 물에 탄 옥수수전분 1테이블스푼을 섞는다. 닭 가슴살을 유리접시나 볼에 넣고 양념장을 넣는다. 잘 섞어준 후 그릇 뚜껑을 덮어서 냉장고에 30분 동안 보관한다.

❷ 소스 : 작은 볼에 와인 1테이블스푼, 간장소스 1테이블스푼, 오일 1테이블스푼, 물에 탄 옥수수전분 1테이블스푼, 매운 칠리 페이스트, 식초 그리고 설탕을 넣고 섞는다. 그 다음 파, 마늘, 통조림, 밤 그리고 땅콩을 넣는다. 그리고 중간 크기의 냄비에 넣고 천천히 좋은 향이 날 때까지 끓여준다.

❸ 그 후 미리 준비해 둔 양념된 고기를 큰 프라이팬에 넣고 고기가 하얀색이 되고 국물이 날아가도록 재빨리 볶아준다. 소스향이 나면, 볶아놓은 닭을 넣고 소스가 걸쭉해질 때까지 약한 불에서 살짝 조리한다.

Phat Thai
(Serving 4)

Ingredients

banh pho 400g

4 large garlic cloves, finely chopped

1 small bunch coriander

50ml vegetable oil

200g raw prawns, peeled

85g pickled turnips, chopped (optional)

1 Tbsp sugar

3 eggs, beaten

2 Tbsp oyster sauce

2 Tbsp fish sauce

300g bean sprouts

Juice 1 lime

1 bunch spring onions, sliced on the diagonal

100g roasted peanuts, crushed

3 red chillies, deseeded and finely chopped

Directions

❶ Soak the noodles in cold water for up to 2 hrs, then drain and set aside. Using a pestle and mortar, pound the garlic with the chopped coriander stems or roots.

❷ Heat the oil in a wok over a high heat. When shimmering, add the garlic and coriander mix. Stir for a few moments, then add the prawns and pickled turnip, if using. Cook for 30 secs, then add the sugar. Add the noodles and stir for 1 min, making sure everything is well mixed. Add the eggs and cook for 2 mins more.

❸ Pour in the oyster and fish sauce, then add the bean sprouts, lime juice, most of the spring onions, most of the roasted peanuts and most of the chilli. Toss and cook for around 2 minutes, then serve scattered with coriander and the rest of the chilli, peanuts and spring onions.

Vocabulary

1.	banh pho	반-포(쌀국수)
2.	garlic cloves	통마늘
3.	coriander	고수(중국 파슬리라고 불리는 허브의 일종)
4.	turnip	무
5.	bean sprout	콩나물(여기서는 '숙주'를 뜻함)
6.	pestle	절구
7.	mortar	절구통
8.	wok	웍(중국 음식을 볶거나 요리할 때 쓰는 우묵하게 큰 냄비)
9.	scatter	뿌리다
10.	soak	물에 흠뻑 적시다

재료

두껍고 마른 타이식 쌀국수 400g
잘게 다진 통마늘 4개
작은 코리앤더 1묶음(줄기와 뿌리는 다지고 잎은 따로 보관)

식물성 기름 50ml

껍질 벗긴 생대하 200g

썬 무 85g(선택사항 : 무피클 다진 것 85g)

설탕 1티스푼

깬 달걀 3개

굴소스 2티스푼

생선소스 2티스푼

숙주나물 300g

라임 1개 분량의 주스

어슷하게 자른 파 1개

구워서 빻은 땅콩 100g

씨 빼고 잘게 다진 빨간 칠리(고추) 3개

만드는 법

❶ 면을 찬물에 2시간 동안 담갔다가 물기를 빼서 놔둔다. 마늘과 다져놓은 고수줄기와 뿌리를 넣고 작은 절구와 절구통을 이용해서 빻는다.

❷ 웍에 기름을 두르고 센 불에 가열한다. 가열되면 마늘과 고수 섞은 것을 넣는다. 몇 번 저어준 후 대하와 무를 넣는다. 30초 정도 조리 후 설탕을 넣는다. 그 후 면을 넣고 1분 동안 모든 것이 잘 섞이도록 저어준다. 마지막으로 계란을 넣고 2분 더 조리한다.

❸ 굴소스와 생선소스를 붓고, 숙주나물, 라임주스, 파, 구운 땅콩 그리고 칠리고추를 넣는다. 섞으면서 2분 정도 더 조리한 후 나머지 고수, 칠리고추, 땅콩 그리고 파를 뿌린다.

Sauerbraten
(Serving 4)

![Ingredients icon] Ingredients

2 teaspoons salt

1 teaspoon ground ginger

1 (4 pound) beef top round roast

2½ cups water

2 cups cider vinegar

2 ea medium onions, sliced

1/3 cup sugar

2 tablespoons mixed pickling spice

1 teaspoon whole peppercorns

8 ea whole cloves

2 pc bay leaves

2 tablespoons vegetable oil

1/4 ea gingersnaps, crushed

 Directions

① Combine salt and ginger; rub over roast. Place in a deep glass bowl. In a saucepan, combine water, vinegar, onions, sugar, pickling spices, peppercorns, cloves and bay leaves; bring to a boil. Pour over roast; turn to coat. Cover and refrigerate for 2 days, turning twice a day.

② Remove roast, reserving marinade; pat roast dry. In a large kettle or Dutch oven, brown roast on all sides in oil over medium-high heat. Strain marinade, reserving half of the onions and seasonings. Pour 1 cup of marinade and reserved onions and seasonings over roast (cover and refrigerate remaining marinade). Bring to a boil. Reduce heat; cover and simmer for 3 hours or until meat is tender.

③ Strain cooking liquid, discarding the onions and seasonings. Measure liquid; if necessary, add enough reserved marinade to equal 3 cups. Pour into a saucepan; bring to a rolling boil. Add gingersnaps; simmer until gravy is thickened. Slice roast and serve with gravy.

Vocabulary

1.	vinegar	식초
2.	peppercorn	통후추
3.	bay leaf	월계수잎
4.	gingersnap	생강과 당밀로 맛을 낸 작은 쿠키
5.	marinade	양념에 절이다
6.	Dutch oven	철제 냄비
7.	gravy	육즙으로 만든 소스

 재료

소금 2티스푼
생강 간 것 1티스푼
겉만 구워진 소고기 1(4파운드)

물 2½컵
식초 2컵
썬 양파 2개
설탕 1/3컵
섞은 피클링스파이스 2테이블스푼
통후추 1티스푼
정향 8알
월계수잎 2장
식물성 기름 2테이블스푼
빻아둔 생강쿠키 1/4개

🥣 만드는 법

❶ 소금과 생강을 섞어서 고기에 문지른 후 깊이가 있는 유리 그릇(bowl)에 담는다. 소스팬에 물, 식초, 양파, 설탕, 피클링스파이스, 통후추, 정향 그리고 월계수잎을 넣고 섞은 후 끓인다. 고기(roast)에 그 소스를 붓고 뒤집어준다. 뚜껑을 덮고 냉장고에 2일간 보관한다. 그리고 하루에 2번씩 뒤집는다.

❷ 고기를 뺀 후, 양념을 따로 보관한다. 고기를 말린다. 고기를 큰 냄비나 철제 냄비에 넣고 중간보다 센 열로 모든 면이 갈색이 되도록 굽는다. 양파와 양념을 반을 남기고 나머지 반만 체에 거른다. 재워뒀던 양념 1컵과 양파를 고기에 붓고 끓이다가 불을 줄이고 3시간 또는 고기가 연해질 때까지 조리한다.

❸ 국물이 줄어들면 양파와 양념을 버린다. 필요하다면 양념을 3컵 정도 되게 더 넣는다. 소스팬에 붓고 생강쿠키를 넣어서 육즙소스(gravy)가 걸쭉해질 때까지 끓인다. 고기를 자르고 그레이비 소스를 곁들여 낸다.

Chapter 3

한국음식 소개 회화

ABC Hotel의 새로운 외국인 총주방장(Executive Chef)이 한국에 왔습니다. 다음은 같은 호텔에 근무하는 한국인 셰프(Chef Kim)가 그를 위해 다양한 한국 음식을 소개하는 내용입니다. 맛있는 한국 음식을 표현하는 방법을 잘 익혀서 활용해 봅시다.

1 Bulgogi

오늘은 외국인 셰프가 이미 한 번 먹어본
불고기와 김치에 대해서 이야기를 나누고
그 음식들에 대한 설명을 합니다.
그럼 먼저 불고기부터...

Vocabulary and Expressions

be interested in	~에 관심(흥미)이 있다
cuisine	요리
introduce	소개하다
explain	설명하다
delicious	맛있는
In fact	사실은
My pleasure	저의 기쁨이죠(You're welcome의 뜻으로 쓰임)
a little bit	조금, 약간
spicy	매운
Why don't we(you)~	'~하는 게 어때요?'라고 하는 권유의 표현법
marinated	미리 양념을 해서 재워 놓은
thinly sliced	얇게 저민
seasoning	양념
pan fry	프라이팬에서 전 부치듯이 굽는 것

(E : Executive Sous Chef, K : Chef Kim)

K : Hi, chef! I'm glad to hear you're interested in Korean cuisine.

E : Oh, yes, very much! Do you mind introducing and explaining some great Korean dishes?

K : No, not at all. In fact, I'll be more than glad to show and explain our delicious food.

E : Oh, thank you!

K : My pleasure! By the way, have you tried any Korean dishes so far?

E : Yes, a couple of dishes. I had Bulgogi and Kimchi.

K : Really? Good for you! What did you think of them?

E : Well, Bulgogi was great and Kimchi was a little bit spicy. Can you tell me more about them?

K : Sure! Why don't we start with Bulgogi. It is grilled marinated beef.
You prepare thinly sliced beef and put some soy sauce, garlic, sesame seed oil, pepper, and sugar for seasoning. Then leave it for a few hours to grill or pan fry it just before you eat.

E : Sounds pretty simple. I'll have to make it sometime. Can you help?

K : Certainly! Before you try, let's go and have some Bulgogi. I know a great Bulgogi place.

E : Great!

Mind는 '꺼리다'라는 뜻을 가진 동사로서 뒤에는 ~ing형이 와야 한다. 이 동사 뒤에는 'to' 부정사를 쓸 수 없다.

또한, 'Do you mind~'는 '~을 꺼리십니까'라는 일종의 부정 의문문이기 때문에 항상 'Not at all'이나 'No'라고 대답해야 '~꺼리지 않는다'라는 긍정의 뜻이 된다.

예) Do you mind smoking outside? (밖에서 담배를 피워주시겠어요?)
    No, not at all. (네, 그렇게 하겠습니다.)

2 Kimchi

'불고기'와 같이 이미 외국인 셰프가 맛본 '김치'에 대해서 국민 음식이라고 소개하고 간단하게 만드는 법과 김치 저장하는 법에 대해서도 설명합니다.

Vocabulary and Expressions

unique taste	독특한 맛
national dish	국민 음식
fermented	발효된
fridge	냉장고(refrigerator의 줄임말)
variety	다양함, 다양성
seasoning	양념
room temperature	실온
prefer	더 선호하다

K : Chef, before we get to the Bulgogi restaurant, let's talk about "Kimchi" this time.

E : Yes, that's a great idea. I think it has a unique taste to it. Can you tell me more about it?

K : Sure. Kimchi is Korea's national dish. It is a traditional fermented Korean dish made of vegetables with a variety of seasonings. You can make hundreds of varieties made with a main vegetable ingredient such as napa cabbage, radish, scallion, or cucumber.

E : Is that so? How interesting!

K : After you make Kimchi, leave it in room temperature one or two days so that it can start to ferment and then keep it in a fridge or Kimchi fridge.

E : I see. When I tasted Kimchi, it was rather spicy. Is it always that spicy?

K : Well, most Koreans love to eat hot and spicy food. So we prefer spicy Kimchi, but you can make non-spicy one.

영어로 '먹다'라는 표현을 할 때는 영어 단어 'eat'를 먼저 떠 올립니다. 하지만 'have'를
사용하는 것이 훨씬 자연스러울 때가 더 많다는 사실을 기억하시기 바랍니다.

예) '아침밥을 먹었습니다' ➜ I had breakfast.로 표현하는 것이 좋습니다.

3 Samgyetang

한국요리는 모두 맵고 자극적이라고 생각할 수도 있는 외국 사람들의 선입견을 없애기 위해서 '삼계탕'을 소개하고 설명합니다.

Vocabulary and Expressions

Indeed	정말로 그렇군요
tradition	전통
whole	전체, 통째로
widely recognized as	~로 널리 알려져 있다
be stuffed with	~으로 속을 채우다
energy boosting meal	원기회복 보양식
Besides	그 외에도
mild dish	부드러운, 자극적이지 않은, 맵거나 짜지 않은 음식
sticky rice	찹쌀
treat	대접하다

K : Hi, chef! It's very hot today, isn't it?

E : Indeed!

K : In Korea, it is our tradition to have a chicken on a hot day like this.

E : Is that so? What kind of chicken dish do you have?

K : We usually have a dish called "Samgyetang". It is a whole young chicken stuffed with ginseng, sticky rice, jujubes (Korean dates), and garlic. It is widely recognized as an energy-boosting meal during the summer.

E : Sounds great!

K : Besides it is a mild dish, so anyone who doesn't like spicy food, they'd love it.

E : I'm glad to hear that.

K : Would you like to try it?

E : I'd love to.

K : All right. Let me treat you with a nice Samgyetang, then.

E : Really? Thank you!

4 Bibimbap

외국인 셰프가 우리나라의 '나물'에 대해서
물어봅니다. 나물에 대해서 먼저 설명하고
나물이 주재료인 '비빔밥'을 소개합니다.

Vocabulary and Expressions

blanched	데친
depend on	~에 의존하다
variety of vegetables	다양한 채소
literally	문자 그대로
be called	~라고 불린다
signature dish	대표 음식
be served as	(음식이) ~로 나오다
be stirred together	~와 같이 섞는다(비빈다)
raw	날것의, 익히지 않은
ingredients	(요리) 재료들
thoroughly	완전히, 철저하게
Exactly	바로 그거야!

E : Hi, Mr. Kim! Do you have a minute? I have a question for you.

K : Yes, chef. You can ask me anything.

E : Good! What is 'Namul'?

K : Oh, Namul? It is blanched or stir-fried vegetables seasoned in various ways.
Back in old days in Korea, they didn't have enough meat for people, so they
depended on variety of vegetables that were largely available.

E : I see.

K : Well, the most famous 'Namul' dish is called 'Bibimbap'. The word literally
means "mixed rice". It is a signature Korean dish.

E : Sounds interesting!

K : Bibimbap is served as a bowl of warm white rice topped with namul that are sauteed and seasoned vegetables and Gochujang (chili pepper paste). A raw or fried egg and sliced meat, usually beef, are common additions. The ingredients are stirred together thoroughly just before eating.

E : It sounds really healthy, though.

K : Exactly! Also, it can be served either cold or hot.

E : Is it difficult to make?

K : No, not at all. Why don't I show you how to make it?

E : Would you? That'd be great!

5 Japchae

한국인 셰프가 외국인 셰프를 할머니 생신날
집으로 초대하는 내용입니다.
그날 생일잔치에 오면 여러 가지
한국 요리를 맛볼 수 있다고 말하고
'잡채'에 대해 소개하고 있습니다.

Vocabulary and Expressions

invite	초대하다
honor	영광
traditional	전통적인
including	~을 포함한
be comfortable	~하기에 편안하다(불편함이 없다)
I'm trying	노력 중이다
various	다양한
authentic	진짜
shredded	길게 자른
typically	전형적으로(일반적으로)
flavor	맛, 맛을 내다
sweeten with	~으로 단맛을 내게 하다
slippery	미끄러운

K : Hi, chef! Are you busy on next Friday?

E : No, I don't think so. But Why?

K : That's my grandmother's birthday. So I'd like to invite you.

E : Really? Thank you!

K : My mother is going to make a lot of traditional Korean dishes including
   Bulgogi, Kimchi, lots of Namul, Japchae and so on. You can try authentic
   Korean dishes at our home.

E : Thank you! It's an honor to be invited at your grandmother's birthday party.

K : My pleasure! By the way, are you comfortable with chopsticks now?

E : I'm trying.

K : The reason why I'm asking is that the one dish my mother is cooking 'Japchae'.

E : What is it?

K : It is a Korean dish made from sweet potato noodles—called dangmyeon, stir fried in sesame oil with various vegetables, typically thinly sliced carrots, onion, spinach, and mushrooms, and shredded beef or pork. You can flavor them with soy sauce and sweeten with sugar. It is usually served garnished with sesame seeds and slivers of chili. It is really delicious but the noodles can be slippery for you to pick up with chopsticks.

E : I guess I need to practice a lot.

K : Don't worry. We'll prepare a fork for you, just in case.

6 Sundubu Jjigae

한국인 셰프가 추운 겨울날 한국인들이 즐기는 '순두부'를 외국인 셰프에게 소개하고 설명합니다.

Vocabulary and Expressions

so far	지금까지
be used to	~에 익숙하다
be great for	~에 아주 좋다
stew dish	우리나라의 찌개와 유사함
made with	~로 만들다
instead of	~ 대신에
hot pepper paste	고추장
hot pepper powder	고춧가루

K : Hi, chef! It's snowing. How do you like Korean winter so far?

E : I like it because I'm used to this kind of cold weather. And I love snow.

K : Me, too! It snows a lot this winter. I think Sundubu is great for cold weather like today. Have you heard about it?

E : No, I haven't. What is it?

K : It's a hot and spicy Korean stew dish made with soft soybean curd, various seafood like oysters, mussels, clams and shrimps, vegetables, mushrooms, onion, scallions, hot pepper paste and hot pepper powder. Then, a raw egg is put in the stew while it is still boiling. This dish is eaten with a bowl of cooked white rice and several side dishes like Kimchi and Namul. Also, you can put meat, if you like, instead of seafood.

E : Sounds delicious but pretty hot, I'm afraid.

K : Yes, it is. It's spicy but very good. Would you like to try?

E : Why not? Let's go for it!

PART Ⅲ

Chapter 1

영어 기초문법 다지기

Ⅰ. 영어의 2가지 동사 종류

A. Be동사

- 우리나라 말로는 주로 '~입니다'라고 해석됩니다.
- 어떤 상태를 나타낼 때 사용합니다.

> 예) 나는 학생입니다. I <u>am</u> a student.
> 그는 요리사입니다. He <u>is</u> a cook.
> 그녀는 바쁩니다. She <u>is</u> busy.

- 주어에 따라 아래 표와 같이 형태가 바뀝니다.

I *am*	we *are*
you *are*	you *are*
he/she/it *is*	they *are*

 연습문제

알맞은 'be'동사를 넣으시오. (현재형)

1. I _____ 21 years old.
2. My mother ____ a nurse.
3. My brother ____ a good cook.
4. His dad _____ a lawyer.
5. Terry and I _____ good friends.
6. This bag ____ heavy.
7. These bags _____ heavy.
8. He _____ interested in music.
9. The stores _____ open today.
10. It ___ sunny.

* 정답은 p.170 참조.

B. 일반동사(혹은 'Do동사'라 불림)

- 영어의 'be'동사를 제외한 모든 동사 : think, get, meet, start, go, give, write, need, shout, tell... etc.

- *be*동사 이외의 일반적인 동사를 말하며 특히 <u>주의해야 할 점은</u>

1) 주어가 3인칭일 때

> **핵심 포인트!**
>
> 3인칭은 영어 단어의 I, You를 제외한 모든 단수 인칭을 뜻합니다.
> 예) I - 1인칭(나)
>   You - 2인칭('당신' 또는 '여러분')
>   Suzi - 3인칭('나'와 '너' '여러분'을 뺀 나머지 모두가 3인칭임!)
>   My mother - 3인칭(1인칭 아님 X)
>   Your brother - 3인칭(2인칭 아님 X)
>   They - 3인칭 복수(단수 아님 X)
>   Tom and his sister - 3인칭 복수

2) 단수이고(1사람 또는 1개)

3) 시제가 현재일 때에는 <u>반드시</u> 동사에 -(*e*)*s*를 붙입니다.

예를 들어, 'The orientation starts at 10:00'이라는 문장이 있을 때, 여기서 The orientation은 3인칭 단수이므로 start라는 일반동사에 반드시 's'를 붙여야 완벽한 하나의 문장이 됩니다.

자, 그러면 비슷한 연습문제를 풀어볼까요~

연습문제

주어진 동사를 알맞게 변화시켜 넣으시오. (현재형)

1. I _____ in an office. (work)
2. He _____ in an office. (work)
3. I _____ in Canada. (live)
4. Susan _____ in Canada. (live)
5. It _____ a lot in summer. (rain)
6. The earth _____ around the sun. (go)
7. The ABC bank _____ at 9:00am in the morning. (open)
8. The banks _____ at 9:00am in the morning. (open)
9. Peter _____ a shower every morning. (take)
10. We _____ a shower every morning. (take)

* 정답은 p.170 참조.

의문문 만들기

A. Be동사 의문문

앞에서 배운 Be동사를 의문문으로 바꾸기는 무척 쉽습니다. 의문문은 간단히 주어와 동사의 위치만 바꾸면 됩니다.

예) She is beautiful. ➔ Is she beautiful?

이제 아래 문제를 풀어볼까요?

연습문제

먼저 각 문장에 적합한 'be'동사를 넣어 문장을 완성한 후 그 문장을 의문문으로 바꾸시오.

1. I _____ 21 years old. ➔
2. My mother _____ a nurse. ➔
3. My brother _____ a good cook. ➔
4. His dad _____ a lawyer. ➔
5. Terry and I _____ good friends. ➔
6. This bag _____ heavy. ➔
7. These bags _____ heavy. ➔
8. He _____ interested in music. ➔
9. The stores _____ open today. ➔
10. It ___ sunny. ➔

* 정답은 p. 170 참조.

B. 일반동사 의문문 만들기

be동사와 달리 일반동사는 조동사의 도움을 받아야 합니다.

- 1인칭(I), 2인칭(You)과 복수형(2사람 또는 2개 이상을 뜻함) : Do 사용
- 3인칭, 단수, 현재형은 : Does 사용

예) I live in Seoul. → **Do** you live in Seoul?
He lives in Seoul. → **Does** he live in Seoul?

 **연습문제(1)**

다음 각 문장에 Do 또는 Does를 넣으시오.

1. _____ you know my friend Andy?
2. _____ this bus go to ABC University?
3. _____ you speak Chinese?
4. _____ Tom go to work on Saturdays?
5. _____ this store sell stamps?
6. _____ Bill and Harry play golf?
7. _____ you play the piano?
8. _____ Suzi work in a restaurant?
9. _____ we need more eggs?
10. _____ this bus go to Kangnam?

* 정답은 p. 170 참조.

 연습문제(2)

아래 문장을 의문문을 만드시오.

1. Ann teaches English. _____
2. The professors know her. _____
3. You play the piano. _____
4. John works in a restaurant. _____
5. We need more eggs. _____
6. Mary likes parties. _____
7. They smoke. _____
8. This train stops at Daegu. _____
9. Harry and Jinsu play golf. _____
10. She wants to go home. _____

* 정답은 p. 170 참조.

Lesson 3

영어의 의문문

A. 영어에는 기본적으로 'Yes-No questions'와 'Wh-questions' 등 2종류의 의문문이 있습니다.

먼저 'Yes-No questions'란 대답할 때 반드시 'yes'나 'no'로 대답해야 합니다. 이해하기는 쉽지만 실천하기는 그리 만만치 않습니다.

1. Are you feeling OK? _____, I'm fine, thanks.
2. Is it raining outside? _____, take an umbrella.
3. Are they Australians? _____, they are Canadians.
4. Does he work today? _____, he is off today.
5. Do we need to go there? _____, I believe so.

B. Wh-questions란 Wh는 Who, When, Where, What, Why와 How를 일컫는 말로써 우리나라에서는 육하원칙이라고 칭하는 것입니다. 이러한 의문사를 가지고 의문문을 만들 경우에는 그에 해당하는 답변을 하면 됩니다.

잠깐~!

Why로 질문을 받으면, 반드시 Because로 문장을 시작해야 하는 점도 잊지 마세요!

연습문제

---

1. Who cooked this spaghetti? I _____.
2. When is your birthday? It is _____. (5월 20일)
3. What did you do yesterday? I _____ __ _____. (영화를 보았습니다)
4. Where did you watch the movie? I watched at a _____ _____. (ABC Cinema에서 보았습니다.)
5. How did you get there? I _____. (걸어갔습니다)
6. Why did you go there? Because it is _____ to my home. (가깝다)

자, 이제 이해 되셨나요?

---

* 정답은 p.171 참조.

1. 영어의 동사 변화

영어의 동사는 시제에 따라 형태가 바뀝니다. 따라서 어제, 일주일 전, 몇 년 전 등의 지나간 기간에 대해서 말할 때는 동사를 과거시제 형태로 사용해야 합니다.

A. Be동사의 과거시제는 아래 표와 같이 변한다.

단수형			복수형		
I He She It My dog	→	Was	We You They My friends Sue and I	→	Were

예를 들면

1) am/is(현재) → was(과거)로 바꿀 경우,

- I <u>am</u> tired(현재) → I <u>was</u> tired last night.(과거)
- Where <u>is</u> Linda?(현재) → Where <u>was</u> Linda yesterday?(과거)

2) are(현재)

- You are late.(현재) → You were late yesterday.(과거)
- They aren't here.(현재) → They weren't here last week.(과거)

이제 이 규칙에 따라 문제를 풀어볼까요?

연습문제

아래 문장 ___ 안에 알맞은 'be'동사의 <u>과거형</u>을 넣으시오.

1. Mina ____ 21 last year, so she is 22 now.

2. When he ____ a child, he ____ afraid of dogs.

3. We ____ hungry after the trip, but we ____ ____ tired.

4. The hotel ____ comfortable, but it ____ expensive.

5. Those glasses are nice. ____ they expensive?

6. Why ____ you late the morning?

7. Today the weather ____ nice, but yesterday it ____ very cold.

8. In summer 2000 I ____ in New York.

9. I can't find my car key. It ____ here this morning.

10. My mother ____ a singer when she ____ young.

* 정답은 p. 171 참조.

B. 일반동사의 과거시제

일반동사를 과거시제로 만드는 데는 2가지 방법이 있습니다. 규칙적으로 변하는 동사와 불규칙적으로 변하는 동사가 있기 때문입니다. 먼저 구체적인 방법을 살펴보기로 합시다.

1) 규칙동사

이름 그대로 규칙적으로 변화하는 동사를 말하며 다행히도 영어동사의 대부분은 여기에 속한다. 예를 들면,

work – worked	dance – danced
clean – cleaned	stay – stayed
start – started	need – needed

위의 동사들과 같이 대부분의 일반동사들은 '–ed'를 붙이면 과거형이 된다.

연습문제

아래 주어진 동사를 <u>과거형</u>으로 바꾸시오.

1. I _____ my teeth this morning. (brush)
2. Tim _____ in a bank from 2005 to 2011. (work)
3. It _____ yesterday. (rain)
4. We _____ the party last night. (enjoy)
5. I _____ tennis last weekend. (play)
6. Mina _____ to school yesterday. (walk)
7. I _____ the bathtub the other day. (clean)
8. My brother and I _____ TV all day yesterday. (watch)
9. They _____ up all night. (stay)
10. The store _____ at 9:00 PM last night. (close)

* 정답은 p. 171 참조.

그러나 이런 규칙동사에도 약간의 변형이 있기도 합니다.

〈변형 유형 1〉

- try, study, copy 같이 -y로 끝나는 동사들은 y를 i로 바꾸고 -ed를 붙여야 한다.

  try, study, copy ➜ tried, studied, copied로 바꾼다.

  그러나 enjoy는 그냥 -ed만 붙인다. ➜ enjoyed

〈변형 유형 2〉

아래 유형은 마지막 자음이 되풀이되고 그 다음에 -ed를 붙인다.

- stop ➜ stopped
- plan ➜ planned
- prefer ➜ preferred

2) 불규칙동사

이 동사들은 위와는 반대로 불규칙적으로 변화하는 동사들이므로 외워서 사용해야 합니다. 단지 동사의 수가 그리 많지 않아서 한 번 외워두면 대단히 유익하게 쓰입니다. 다음의 불규칙동사표는 자주 쓰이는 최소한의 동사만 고른 것입니다.

〈불규칙동사표〉

단 어	의 미	과 거	과거완료	단 어	의 미	과 거	과거완료
spend	소비하다, 보내다.	spent	spent	throw	던지다.	threw	thrown
stand	서있다.	stood	stood	fly	날다.	flew	flown
sting	찌르다.	stung	stung	drive	운전하다.	drove	driven
win	이기다.	won	won	ride	(말, 차를) 타다.	rode	ridden
wind [waind]	감다.	wound [waund]	wound [waund]	rise	일어서다, 뜨다.	rose	risen
wound [wund]	상처 입히다.	wounded	wounded	write	쓰다.	wrote	written
strike	치다, 부딪치다.	struck	struck	bite	물다.	bit	bitten
be (am, are, is)	이다, 있다.	was, were	been	hide	숨다.	hid	hidden
do(does)	하다.	did	done	eat	먹다.	ate	eaten
go	가다.	went	gone	give	주다.	gave	given
see	보다.	saw	seen	fall	떨어지다.	fell	fallen
saw	톱질하다.	sawed	sawed	fell	넘어뜨리다.	felled	felled
sow	씨뿌리다.	sowed	sowed	beat	치다.	beat	beat(beaten)
sew	바느질하다.	sewed	sewed	break	깨뜨리다.	broke	broken
bear	낳다.	bore	born	choose	선택하다.	chose	chosen
bear	참다.	bore	borne	freeze	얼다.	froze	frozen
tear	찢다.	tore	torn	get	얻다.	got	got (gotten)
wear	입다.	wore	worn	forget	잊다.	forgot	forgot (forgotten)
begin	시작하다.	began	begun	speak	말하다.	spoke	spoken
drink	마시다.	drank	drunk (drunken)	wake	(잠이) 깨다.	woke	woken
ring	울리다.	rang	rung	steal	훔치다.	stole	stolen
sing	노래하다.	sang	sung	weave	짜다.	wove	woven
swim	수영하다.	swam	swum	lie	눕다.	lay	lain
blow	불다.	blew	blown	lay	눕히다.	laid	laid
draw	그리다.	drew	drawn	shake	흔들다.	shook	shaken
grow	자라다.	grew	grown	take	가져가다.	took	taken
know	알다.	knew	known	show	보여주다.	showed	shown

'불규칙 동사표'를 참고하여 아래 문제를 연습해 볼까요?

연습문제

아래 주어진 동사를 과거형으로 바꾸시오.

1. I _____ this computer yesterday. (buy)
2. My brother _____ home late last night. (come)
3. She _____ a letter to him a week ago. (write)
4. Jerry _____ to London the other day. (fly)
5. I _____ Mina on the street yesterday afternoon. (see)
6. Harry _____ late last night. (work)
7. Bill _____ where I was. (know)
8. Sam _____ a swimming pool at his backyard. (build)
9. We _____ Spanish together. (speak)
10. He _____ French lesson at high school. (take)

* 정답은 p. 171 참조.

Ⅰ. 미래시제

영어에는 미래를 나타낼 때 사용하는 몇 가지 방법이 있습니다만 여기서는 간단하게 2가지만 알아보겠습니다.

1. be going to 'going to' 다음에는 동사의 원형이 옵니다.	I __am__ really __going to__ stop smoking.
2. will 'will' 같은 조동사 뒤에는 동사의 원형이 옵니다.	She __will return__ home tomorrow.

'be going to'와 'will'은 모두 다 미래를 나타내는 방법이지만, 약간의 차이가 있습니다. 'be going to'는 말하는 사람의 의지를 나타내는 방법입니다. 즉 "I __am going__ __to__ play the piano."라고 말한다면, 이것은 내가 피아노를 치기로 결정했고 그렇게 할 것이라는 본인의 의지가 들어 있다는 뜻입니다. 반면 우리가 흔히 쓰는 'will' 조동사는 나의 의지와는 상관없이 미래를 나타낼 때 많이 쓰는 표현법입니다. 예를 들자면 날씨 같은 것이죠.

예) It __will__ rain tomorrow.

연습문제

아래 문장의 빈칸에 알맞은 미래시제를 넣으시오.

1. I ___ _____ _____ buy some books tomorrow.
2. Sarah ___ _____ ____ sell her car.
3. What ____ you _____ ____ do this weekend?
4. I _____ be in Japan tomorrow.
5. Diana _____ pass the exam.
6. My mother ___ _____ __ post a letter.
7. I ___ _____ ___ cook spaghetti tonight.
8. We _____ have a long vacation this summer.
9. My parents _____ be here tomorrow.
10. The class _____ begin at 9:00 in the morning.

* 정답은 p. 171 참조.

I. 'can'과 'could'를 사용한 정중한 표현법

ex) Could I have your name, please?

A. 위 문장에서와 같이 조동사 'can'과 'could'는 상대방에게 어떤 일을 요구할 때, 혹은 허락을 받고자 할 때 쓰입니다. 이때 'can'보다는 'could'가 좀 더 공손한 표현이며 'could you...?'나 'would you...?'는 둘 다 공손한 표현입니다. 'could you...?'로 물었을 때와 'would you...?'로 물었을 때의 차이는 미묘합니다. 'could you...?'는 '이것을 해주실 의향이 있으십니까?'라는 의도를 가지고 질문할 때 주로 사용되고 'would you...?'는 이것을 해주실 의향이 있는지 그리고 해주시는 것이 가능한지를 묻는 의미가 들어 있습니다.

B. 'may'도 허락을 의미하는 조동사입니다.

ex) May I borrow your pen?
    May I come in?

단, may로 묻는 문장에서는 주어가 'I'나 'we'가 될 수 있으나 'you'는 올 수 없습니다.

ex) May I use your phone? (O)
    May we drop by your office tomorrow? (O)
    May <u>you</u> pass the salt? (X)

C. 형식 :

조동사				
can could may	+	주어	+	본동사

이제, 연습문제를 풀어볼까요?

A. 아래 문장을 맞게 배열해 보세요.

1. I, your, have, name, may?

_____

2. show, your, could, you, passport, me?

_____

3. I, can, now, go?

_____

4. sir, would, like, you, a, menu, see, to?

_____

5. your, may, I, take, coat?

_____

6. turn, the, you, could, down, music?

_____

B. 아래 두 문장을 읽고 'May'나 'could'가 들어가는 공손한 표현으로 바꾸어 보세요. 괄호 안에 있는 동사를 이용하세요.

예)

1. I'm your teacher. You want to leave class early. (leave)

   ➜ May I leave class early?

2. You and I are friends. You want to borrow a book from me. (borrow)

_____

3. You are a receptionist at a hotel. You want to know how to spell guest's last name. (spell)

_____

4. You are at the restaurant. You want to take a look at the wine list. (see)

_____

5. You are a librarian. You need to see student's ID for the check-out procedure. (see)

_____

6. You are a waitress at a restaurant. You want to know if the guest wants to sit at a smoking or non-smoking section. (like)

_____

* 정답은 p. 171 참조.

p. 156

1. am	2. is	3. is	4. is	5. are
6. is	7. are	8. is	9. are	10. is

p. 157

1. work	2. works	3. live	4. lives	5. rains
6. goes	7. opens	8. open	9. takes	10. take

p. 158

1. is → Is he 21 years old?
2. is → Is your mother a nurse?
3. is → Is your mother a good cook?
4. is → Is his dad a lawyer?
5. are → Are Terry and you good friends?
6. is → Is this bag heavy?
7. are → Are these bags heavy?
8. is → Is he interested in music?
9. are → Are the stores open today?
10. is → Is it sunny?

p. 159(1)

1. Do	2. Does	3. Do	4. Does	5. Does
6. Do	7. Do	8. Does	9. Do	10. Does

p. 159(2)

1. Does Ann teach English?
2. Does the professor know her?
3. Do you play the piano?
4. Does John work in a restaurant?
5. Do we need more eggs?
6. Does Mary like parties?
7. Do they smoke?
8. Does this train stop at Daegu?
9. Do Harry and Jinsu play golf?
10. Does she want to go home?

p. 160

1. did   2. May 20th   3. saw a movie   4. ABC cinema 5. walked
6. close

p. 162

1. was   2. was, was   3. were, were not 4. was, was   5. are
6. were   7. is, was   8. was   9. was   10. was, was

p. 163

1. brushed   2. worked   3. rained   4. enjoyed   5. played
6. walked   7. cleaned   8. watched   9. stayed   10. closed

p. 166

1. bought   2. came   3. wrote   4. flew   5. saw
6. worked   7. knew   8. built   9. spoke   10. took

p. 167

1. am going to 2. is going to   3. are/going to   4. will   5. will
6. is going to   7. am going to 8. will   9. will   10. will

p. 169

A

1. May I have your name?
2. Could you show me your passport?
3. Can I go now?
4. Would you like to see a menu, sir?
5. May I take your coat?
6. Could you turn down the music?

B

2. May I borrow your book?
3. Could you spell your last name, please?
4. Can I see the wine list, please?
5. May I see your ID(identification) card, please?
6. Would you like to sit at smoking or non-smoking section?

Chapter 2

공항수속, 호텔, 레스토랑 회화

1. Immigration(이민국 심사대에서)

You left the airplane and now you are on your way to the immigration section. Stand in line and prepare your passport, visa, and customs declaration form. Be patient.

참고사항

이민국 심사대에서는 가능한 한 정확하게 여행의 목적, 묵을 장소의 주소, 체류기간을 말하는 것이 좋습니다. 우물쭈물하면 쓸데없는 의심을 불러일으킬 수도 있으므로 미리 대답을 준비하셔서 난처한 상황이 일어나지 않도록 예비하세요.

Vocabulary

immigration card	이민국 신고 카드
purpose	목적
return ticket	돌아가는 비행기표
culinary	조리의
suppose	가정하다
stay	체류, 방문기간

(I : Immigration Officer, T : Traveler)

I : May I see your immigration card and passport, please?

T : Sure! Here you are.

I : What's the purpose of your trip?

T : I'm here on a culinary internship program at the Marriott hotel.

I : How long will you stay?

T : About 10 months.

I : Where are you going to stay?

T : I'm going to stay at the Marriott hotel in Norwich, Connecticut.

I : Do you have a return ticket to Korea?

T : Of course. I'm supposed to leave on Oct. 15th.

I : All right. Enjoy your stay.

T : Thank you!

2. Lost Baggage(수화물을 분실하였을 경우)

You went to the designated carousel and waited until the last bag to be dispensed, but still you do not have your baggage. Then you make your way to the claim office. Be calm.

참고사항

수화물을 찾는 곳에서 짐이 도착하지 않는다면 너무 당황하지 말고 차분하게 수화물 신고소에 가서 신고를 하면 됩니다. 신고 후 하루나 이틀 뒤에 본인(여행자)이 묵고 있는 곳으로 수화물을 배달해 주는 것이 관례입니다. 이런 사고는 종종 발생하므로 여행가방에 꼼꼼히 주소를 쓴 Tag 을 달아주는 것이 최선의 예방책이겠죠~.

Vocabulary

baggage	짐/수화물
flight number	비행기편 번호
carousel	짐 내리는 곳(컨베이어 벨트로 순환됨)
file	서류 작성
lost & found	잃어버린 물건보관소
incoming flight	도착하는 비행기편

(P : Passenger, C : Clerk)

P : Excuse me, my baggage is missing. What should I do?

C : Where are you from?

P : I'm from Incheon, Korea.

C : Do you have your flight number?

P : Here it is, flight number is KL 507.

C : KL 507....
Did you check carousel 6?

P : Yes, I did, but I couldn't find my bag.

C : OK, then, let's file it on the Lost & Found.

P : Do you think we can find it? I have everything in there.

C : Don't worry, ma'am. You will get it back.
It may be on the next incoming flight.

3. At Customs(세관 심사대에서)

Now, you have all your baggage and ready to leave the airport. Before you leave you must proceed through the Customs section. Here you will give your declaration form and will be asked questions about the contents of your baggage. You may also be routinely selected

to be screened. Meaning, be prepared to open all your baggage. It is not that they are picking on you, but it is a normal procedure. Be patient, be calm.

참고사항

이제 짐도 찾고 공항을 떠날 준비가 되었죠? 그러나 떠나기 전에 반드시 세관 검사를 받으셔야죠. 세관 직원으로부터 짐에 관한 질문을 받게 될 것입니다. 또 랜덤으로 관례적인 짐 검사를 받을 수도 있습니다. 항상 준비가 되어 있어야 한다는 뜻입니다. 세관 직원이 당신을 괴롭히려고 그러는 것은 아니고 그들은 그들의 임무를 수행하는 것뿐임을 명심하고 인내하세요. 그리고 침착하세요. 그리고 여행할 때 본인의 몸보다 너무 큰 코트나 재킷은 필요없는 의심을 불러일으킬 수도 있으니 명심하시기 바랍니다.

Vocabulary

customs declaration form	세관 신고서(비행기 안에서 승무원이 도착하기 전에 나누어줌)
declare	신고하다
products	물건, 제품
personal hygiene items	개인 위생용품(치약, 칫솔, 샴푸 등등)
proceed	가다(여기서는 'go'와 같은 개념)
present	보여주다, 내다

(C : Customs Officer, T : Traveler)

C : Please, show me your customs declaration form.

T : Yes, here it is.

C : Do you have anything to declare?

T : No, nothing.

C : Is this all you have?

T : Yes.

C : Are you carrying any fruits or meat products?

T : No, I am not.

C : What's inside this large bag there?

T : Well, I have clothing, books, and personal hygiene items.

C : Please open this bag.

T : Sure.

C : Okay. Proceed to the counter and present your declaration form before leaving.

T : Thank you. Have a nice day.

4. Hotel Check-in

Now, you arrived at your hotel. Check-in at a hotel. is not difficult and hotel staff is usually very friendly. Just prepare your passport and smile.

참고사항

이제 드디어 호텔 체크인을 할 시간입니다. 보통 호텔 직원들은 친절하니까 염려 마시고 여권 등의 신분증을 준비하시고 웃는 얼굴로 호텔 Front Desk로 가셔서 체크인해 볼까요?

Vocabulary

reservation	예약
ocean view	바다전망
account	계좌
facilities	(호텔 내) 각종 시설
leaflet	한 장짜리 작은 안내서
dining	식사
key card	방 열쇠
luggage	짐(여행가방)
colleague	동료

(F : Front Desk Agent, C : Customer)

F : May I help you?

C : Yes, please. I have a reservation. My name is Hankook Kim.

F : Yes, Mr. Kim. How was your flight?

C : A little bit tiring but enjoyable one.

F : Very Good. Well.

F : Oh, yes. Here it is. A single room for three nights with an ocean view. You'll be in room 1012 – that's on the 10th floor. How will you be paying for your account?

C : I'll be paying with my Visa card.

F : Very well.

C : Can you tell me something about the facilities?

F : Yes, this leaflet will show you. It has a map of the city and the hotel. Our Business center is next to the gift shop on this floor.

C : Thank you.

F : Will you be dining here tonight?

C : No, I'll be meeting my colleagues in town.

F : All right. Here is your key card for your room. The bellboy will bring up your luggage to your room in a minute. Enjoy your stay, sir.

C : Thank you!

Tip

호텔방에 들어왔는데 방이 마음에 들지 않을 경우에는 (예 : 담배 냄새 나는 방 / 시끄러운 방 / 청소가 되어 있지 않은 방 등등) Front Desk에 전화해서 room change를 요청하셔도 됩니다. 호텔 고객으로서의 권리이니까요.

5. Room Service-Breakfast Order

Now, you've stayed a night at a comfortable hotel room. You took a shower and feel hungry. You've decided to have breakfast in the room and try to order a room service.

참고사항

편안한 방에서 잠도 잘 자고 샤워도 하고 나니 배가 고프다면 호텔의 room service를 이용해 보는 것도 좋은 방법이겠지요. 요즈음 대부분의 호텔은 24시간 이용가능한 room service가 있습니다. 체크해 보시고 이용해 보는 것도 여행의 맛이겠죠?

Vocabulary

American breakfast	따뜻한 계란요리가 포함된 미국식 아침식사
include	포함하다
scrambled egg	노른자를 터뜨린 계란요리
come with	~와 함께 나오다
Certainly	물론입니다

(G : Guest, R : Room Service Clerk)

G : Good morning, I'd like to have my breakfast in my room. Could you take my order, please?

R : Good morning, sir. Of course, we can take your order now.
   We have an American breakfast and a continental breakfast.
   Which would you prefer?

G : I'd like to have an American breakfast. What is included with the American breakfast?

R : It comes with toast, fruit-juice, cereal, eggs, and coffee or tea.

G : Sounds fine!

R : How would you like your eggs cooked?

G : Scrambled, please.

R : Certainly, sir. Would you like coffee or tea?

G : Coffee, please.

R : Is there anything else, sir?

G : That's all. How long will it take?

R : It will take about 20 minutes, sir.

G : All-right. That's fine. Thank you.

R : Thank you, sir.

6. Taking orders for food 1(음식 주문하기 1)

You're now in a very nice restaurant with your friend. Are you ready to order?

참고사항

외국(특히 북미주에 있는 나라들 : 미국과 캐나다)에서는 웨이터가 손님에게 메뉴를 드린 후 3~4분 후에 와서 손님에게 "주문하시겠어요?"라고 질문하는 것이 일반적입니다. 아직 마음을 정하지 못했다면 시간을 더 달라고 하면 됩니다.

Vocabulary

recommend	추천하다
imported	수입된
daily special	오늘의 특별 기획메뉴
juicy	즙이 많은
mashed	으깬
rare	드문, 보기 힘든, 고기를 겉만 살짝 익힌 상태

(W : Waiter/Waitress, C : Customer, M : Mina)

W : Are you ready to order, sir?

C : Yes. What do you recommend for us tonight?

W : Our daily special is Rib Eye Steak. The meat is imported from Australia and it's sweet and juicy. I'm sure you'll like it, sir.

C : That sounds good. We'll have the daily special, then.

W : How would you like your steak?

C : I'd like to have it medium rare. How about you, Mina?

M : Medium-well, please.

W : How would you like your potatoes?

C : I want mashed potatoes.

M : I'll have French fries, please.

W : Would you like to order dessert now?

C : Well, we'll order it later. Thank you.

W : All right, sir. I'll bring your order in a few minutes. Thank you.

7. Taking orders for food 2(음식 주문하기 2)

You did a fine job in ordering your steak. Now, shall we order different food?

참고사항

미국이나 캐나다의 식당에서는 웨이터가 손님에게 menu를 줄 때, 그날의 special 요리(주로 기획메뉴)에 대해서 설명을 합니다. 잘 들어보시고 그 메뉴를 선택해 보는 것도 좋은 방법이 겠지요. 그리고 웨이터가 음식주문을 받기 전에 꼭 식전음료 주문을 받는 것도 우리나라와는 다른 음식문화입니다.

Vocabulary

ma'am	여성에 대한 존칭
soup of the day	오늘의 수프
mushroom soup	버섯 수프
fish of the day	오늘의 기획 생선요리
sea bass	바다 농어
pan fried	프라이팬에서 구운(전 부치는 방식으로)
garlic sauce	마늘소스
salmon	연어
mushroom	버섯
mineral water	생수

(W : Waiter/Waitress, C : Customer)

W : Good afternoon, ma'am. Here is your menu and wine list. The soup of the day is mushroom and the fish of the day is sea bass. I'll be back to take your order when you're ready. Would you like a drink before your meal?

C : No, I'm fine. Thank you.

(...a few minutes later)

W : Are you ready to order now, ma'am?

C : What's the sea bass like?

W : Oh, that's very nice. It's pan fried and served with garlic sauce.

C : Well, then, I'll have the steak.

W : All right. How would you like that cooked?

C : Medium rare, thanks. Oh, what's that served with?

W : It's served with vegetables and mushroom sauce.

C : That sounds good.

W : So, that's one medium rare steak. Would you care for a side salad?

C : No, thank you. But can I have some more water, please?

W : Certainly, ma'am.

8. Taking orders for drinks 1(음료 주문하기 1)

How about learning how to order wine? They usually have a separate menu for wine in a fine restaurants in the western countries.

참고사항

음료를 주문할 때 다양한 와인은 병이나 잔으로, 맥주는 병으로, hard liquor는 straight나 on-the-rocks로 주문하는 것도 배우셨죠? 이제 음료와 안주도 주문해 볼까요?

Vocabulary

very dry	단맛이 전혀 없는
medium dry	단맛이 약간 있는
instead	대신에
local	현지의
nut	견과
pretzel	프레첼(독일식 마른 과자)
brand	상표

(B : Bartender, C : Customer)

B : What can I get you, sir?

C : Can I have a glass of wine, please?

B : Sure. Red or white?

C : White, please. I'd like a very dry wine.

B : I'm sorry, we're out of very dry whites right now, but we do have a nice medium dry one.

C : Well, then, I'll have a beer instead. Do you have any imported beer?

B : No, I'm sorry. But we do have some great local beers.

C : All right. That will be fine.

B : Will that be all?

C : Do you have any snacks?

B : Of course. We have nuts, pop corns and pretzels.

C : I'll have some pop corns, please.

B : No problem, sir.

9. Taking orders for drinks 2(음료 주문하기 2)

There are so many different kinds of cocktails and beers. Which one would you like to drink?

Vocabulary

a bottle of beer	맥주 한 병
a gin and tonic	진토닉 한 잔
particular	특정한
sweat	땀, 수고('No Sweat'은 'No Problem'과 같은 '문제없다'라는 표현임)

(B : Bartender, C1 : Customer 1, C2 : Customer 2)

B : Good evening, sir. Can I get you anything?

C1 : Let me have a bottle of beer and what about you, John?

C2 : I'll have a gin and tonic, please.

B : Would you care for any particular brand, sir?

C1 : Mmm~ What do you have?

B : We have Heineken, Miller, Budwiser, Mikelob, Coors, Corona, Cass, Asahi, you name it.

C1 : I'll have a miller.

B : And for you, sir? Would you like ice and lemon in your gin and tonic?

C2 : Yes, but can I have lime instead of lemon, please?

B : No sweat, sir.

C2 : Thanks.

10. Dealing with complaints(고객 불평 다루기)

If you are not satisfied with the food they brought for you, you can call your waiter's attention and complain. He/She will take an appropriate action for you.

Vocabulary

rare	덜 익은
chef	주방장
short-staffed	직원이 모자라는
loud	시끄러운
stained	얼룩이 묻은
chipped	(그릇이) 이가 빠진
spicy	매운
mild	부드러운
see to	체크해 보다, 알아보다
at once	즉시
called in sick	병가내다

(W : Waiter/Waitress, C : Customer)

W : Is there anything wrong, sir?

C : Ah, yes, my steak is too rare. I ordered medium rare steak but it's too rare.

W : I'm sorry, sir. I'll take it back to the kitchen and get you another one. I'll make sure it's medium rare this time.

C : Besides, my vegetables are too cold. They are supposed to be warm.

W : I'm very sorry. I'll speak to the chef and bring you some warm vegetables, too.

C : Also, the music is too loud. Could you turn it down?

W : Yes, of course. I'm very sorry for all of these matters, sir.

C : Alright. Thank you for your attention.

Chapter **3**

실용회화(Useful Expressions)

아래의 문장들은 일상생활에서 유익하게 사용할 수 있는 영어 표현들을 간추려본 것입니다. 적극적으로 외워서 활용하면 일상생활에 많은 도움이 될 것입니다.

1. 일상생활

1. 다시 말씀해 주시겠습니까?
   Could you repeat that, please?

2. 천천히 말씀해 주시겠습니까?
   Could you speak slowly, please?

3. 조금 크게 말씀해 주시겠습니까?
   Could you speak a little louder, please?

4. 전화를 잘못 거신 것 같습니다.
   I'm afraid you have the wrong number.

5. 가족 모임을 하다 : ~ have a family reunion (gathering)
   We had a family gathering last weekend at my house.

6. 생일잔치를 하다 : ~ throw (have) a birthday party
   My mom threw a birthday party for my dad.

7. 돌잔치를 하다 : ~ throw(have) a first birthday party
   My cousin threw his son's first birthday party yesterday.

8. 칠순잔치를 하다 : ~ throw(have) the 70th birthday party
   We had my grand father's 70th(seventieth) birthday party at the restaurant.

9. 집들이를 하다 : ~ have a house warming party
   We are planning to have a house warming party on Friday.

10. 제사를 지내다 : ~ perform a ceremony for ancestors
    ~ have a worship ceremony for ancestors
    They had a worship ceremony for their ancestors at their home last night.

11. 지인을 초대하다 : ~ invite acquaintances to the house

He invited many of his friends and acquaintances for his sons first birthday party.

12. 죄송하지만 통화 중입니다.

I'm afraid the line is busy.

13. 저는 홍콩에서 업무상 일이 있습니다.

I am doing some business in Hong Kong.

14. 문제가 없을 겁니다.

This shouldn't be a problem.

15. 그리 어렵지 않을 겁니다.

It shouldn't be too difficult.

16. 가격차이가 얼마입니까?

What's the difference in price?

17. 컴퓨터가 고장났습니다.

The computer is down.

18. 누군가 실수를 한 것이 분명합니다.

There must be a mistake.

19. 제가 사과드립니다.

I do apologize.

20. 비자카드 받습니까?

Do you take Visa?

21. 카드 유효기간이 지났습니다.

Your card has expired.

22. 감사합니다.

I'd appreciate it.

23. 새해 결심이 뭐죠?
    What's your New Year's resolution?

24. 제 심부름 하나 해줄래요?
    Can you run an errand for me?

25. 세상의 긍정적인 면을 보세요.
    Look at the bright side of things.

26. 그 사람을 과소평가하지 마세요.
    Do not underestimate him.

27. 요즘 세상사는 재미가 없어요.
    I have no life these days.

28. 그 사람은 정신이 없어요.
    He's so absent-minded.

29. 절대 안돼요.
    It's out of the question.

30. 문제없어요.
    It doesn't matter.

31. 시간 있어요?
    Do you have time?

32. 지금 몇 시입니까?
    Do you have the time?

33. 관광 안내소가 어디예요?
    Where is the tourist information center?

34. 그 항목을 손님의 계좌에서 지워드리겠습니다.
   I will delete that item from your account immediately.

35. 불편을 끼쳐드려 대단히 죄송합니다.
   I'm very sorry for the inconvenience.

36. 손님, 뭐가 잘못되었습니까?
   Is there anything wrong, ma'am?

37. 성함이 어떻게 되십니까?
   Could I have your name, please?

38. 성함 철자를 불러주시겠습니까?
   Could you spell your last name, please?

39. 제가 즉시 체크해 보겠습니다.
   I'll see to it right away.

40. 제가 그것을 즉시 교체해 드리겠습니다.
   I'll replace it right away.

41. 죄송합니다만, 그런 성함을 가진 고객님은 안 계십니다.
   I'm afraid there's no guest with that name.

42. 백(짐)이 몇 개입니까?
   How many bags do you have?

43. 이 짐을 부치고 싶습니다.
   I would like to check in this bag.

44. 이 작은 가방은 제가 직접 들고 탈 겁니다.
   I want to carry this small bag on the plane.

45. 손님께서는 10시 30분에 첫 번째 탑승 방송을 들으실 겁니다.
You'll hear the first boarding call at 10:30.

46. 그것은 손님께서 직접 들고 가실 건가요?
That's your carry on?

47. 손님이 원하시는 건 무엇이든 꺼낼 수 있습니다.
You can take out whatever you like.

48. 손님의 표와 여권을 보여주시겠습니까?
Could I have your ticket and passport?

49. 그 비행기편에 자리를 하나 만들 수 있을 거예요.
I can get you a seat on that one.

50. 지금 돈을 지불하시겠습니까?
Do you want to pay for it now?

51. 어떤 것이 가능한지 제가 한번 체크해 보겠습니다.
I'll have a look at what's available.

52. 이 비행편에 빈자리가 있습니다.
There are seats available on this flight.

53. 이 비행편은 만석입니다.
The flight is full.

54. 한 자리 예약해 주시겠습니까?
Can you reserve one for me?

4. 식당

55. 음식과 술을 준비하다 : ~ prepare food and drinks
They prepared a lot of food and drinks for the ceremony.

56. 스테이크를 어떻게 구워 드릴까요?
How would you like your steak?

57. 계란은 어떻게 요리해 드릴까요?
How would you like your eggs?

58. 잔으로 하시겠습니까? 병으로 하시겠습니까?
Would you like a glass or a bottle?

59. 얼마나 기다려야 합니까?
How long do I have to wait?

60. 여기에 서명해 주시겠습니까?
Could you sign here, please?

61. 어떻게 요금을 지불하시겠습니까?
How would you like to pay?

62. 신용카드 받습니까?
Do you take credit card?

63. 영수증 여기 있습니다.
Here's your receipt.

64. 제가 다른 것으로 가지고 오겠습니다.
I'll get you another one.

65. 제가 그 음식을 주방으로 가져가겠습니다.
I'll take it back to the kitchen.

66. 오늘밤 종업원이 부족합니다.
We're short-staffed tonight.

67. 이 테이블보는 얼룩이 묻었네요.
The tablecloth is stained.

68. 유리잔이 깨졌네요.
The glass is chipped.

69. 제가 새것으로 가져오겠습니다.
I'll bring you a new one.

70. 공짜 점심은 없다. (모든 것에는 대가가 있다.)
There's no free lunch.

71. 현지 요리가 있나요?
Do you have any local dishes?

72. 같은 걸로 주세요.
Same here, please.

73. 그걸로 할게요.
I'll take it.

74. 완전히 익혀주세요.
Well done, please.

75. 중간 정도 익혀주세요.
Medium, please.

76. 이 요리는 어떻게 조리하죠?
How is this cooked?

77. 디저트는 생략할게요.
I'll skip the dessert.

78. 주문한 게 아직 안 나왔어요.
I didn't get my order yet.

79. 물을 좀 더 주실래요?
May I have some more water, please?

80. 포크를 떨어뜨렸어요.
I dropped my fork.

81. 빵을 좀 더 주세요.
    Some more bread, please.

82. 남은 음식은 싸주실래요?
    Can I have a doggy bag?

83. 여기서 드실 건가요, 가져가실 건가요?
    For here or to go?

84. 빨대 주시겠어요?
    Please give me a straw.

85. 한식과 양식 중 어느 것을 드시고 싶으세요?
    Would you like Korean or Western food?

86. 술 한 잔 할래요?
    Do you want a drink?

87. 오늘은 내가 쏠게!
    It's on me today!

88. 한 잔만 더하자.
    One for the road.

89. 2차 갑시다!
    Let's go barhopping!

90. 얼음을 넣어주세요.
    On the rocks, please.

91. 나눠서 냅시다.
    Let's split the bill.

92. 내가 낼게.
    I'll treat you.

93. 냄새가 좋은데요.
   It smells good.

94. 군침이 도는군요.
   My mouth is watering.

95. 너무 맛있어요. (또는 너무 좋아요.)
   It's out of this world.

96. 난 음식을 가려먹어.
   I'm a picky eater.

97. 난 채식주의자야.
   I'm a vegetarian.

98. 난 매운 음식 좋아해.
   I like hot food.

99. 여기 단골이에요.
   I'm a regular here.

100. 계산서 주세요.
   Check, please.

PART Ⅳ

Chapter 1

영문 이력서 작성

1. Cover Letter 작성법

영문 이력서를 작성할 때, Resume(이력서)에 앞서, 우리나라에는 없는 Cover Letter (커버레터)라는 것이 있습니다. 이것은 우리나라의 자기소개서와 비슷할 것이라고 생각하시는 분들이 간혹 있습니다만, 이 Cover Letter는 절대 우리가 흔히 생각하는 자기소개서가 아닙니다.

이 Cover Letter는 자신이 이 position에 지원하게 된 동기, 왜 본인이 이 일에 적임자인지를 간단하지만 명쾌하게 서술하여 인사 담당자가 뒤에 첨부된 이력서를 읽어보게 하는 것이 목적이므로 장황하게 작성하면 안됩니다. 그러므로 한 페이지 이상 넘기지 않도록 주의합니다.

그리고 Cover Letter가 반드시 Resume 위에 있어야 합니다. 왜냐하면 이것은 일종의 포장지 역할을 한다고 볼 수 있기 때문입니다. 그리고 특별한 일이 없는 이상, Cover Letter는 반드시 resume와 함께 보내야 합니다.

이제, Cover Letter를 구체적으로 살펴볼까요?

Cover Letter는 글자 그대로 본인이 취업하기를 원하는 회사의 인사를 담당하는 분에게 보내는 편지입니다. 그래서 형식도 편지 형식을 따릅니다. 먼저, 날짜, 수신자 성함, 직위, 회사이름과 주소를 적습니다. 그 다음 본론을 약 3-4문단으로 적고 Closing (인사말과 본인 서명)을 하면 끝납니다.

날짜와 주소 부분은 오타가 없는지 확인하시고, 본문(Body)은 크게 세 부분(문단)으로 나누어 작성하면 됩니다.

첫 번째 문단에는 왜 내가 이 Cover Letter를 쓰는지를 밝혀야 합니다. 어디서 모집한다는 소식을 들었는지를 기재하도록 합니다(추천인 이름/신문/광고/인터넷 주소 등등). 그런 후에, 자신이 왜 그 자리에 지원하는지와 적합한 사람인지를 열정/의지를 담아서 표현합니다. 하지만 아주 간단명료하게 적습니다.

두 번째 문단에는 자신이 지금까지 다니고 있는 직장(들)에서 무엇을 성취해 왔는지와 그런 업적들이 어떻게 지원하고자 하는 회사에 도움이 될지를 간략하지만 아주 파워풀하게 피력해야 합니다. 여기에 써진 문장을 보고 뒤에 별첨되어 있는 이력서가 보고 싶어지게 만들어야 하니까요. 이 두 번째 문단이 Cover Letter에서 가장 중요한 부분입니다.

세 번째는 면접 시간과 날짜를 잡기 위해서 정중히 제안을 하는 부분입니다. 연락처를 남기고 먼저 인터뷰를 하자고 적극적으로 제안하는 것이 좋습니다.

이제, 조금 더 구체적으로 살펴봅시다.

1) Cover Letter에 꼭 기재해야 할 사항들

- 날짜 : 월/일/연도 순서로 페이지의 맨 위쪽 왼쪽이나 오른쪽에 씁니다.
  예) 20××, 5월 10일 → May 10th, 20××

- 수신자의 성명과 주소
  - 받는 사람의 성명–이름 앞에 존칭(남자 : Mr./ 여자 : Ms.)을 쓰는 것이 바람직합니다. (예 : Mr. John Doe, 또는 Ms. Amy Smith)
  - 받는 사람의 직함과 부서를 기재합니다.
    예 : Personnel Manager, Human Resources Dept.
  - 회사이름 및 도시, 나라의 순서로 적습니다.
    예 : ○○Company
      Seoul, Korea

- 어디서 모집한다는 소식을 들었는지를 기재하도록 합니다. (추천인 이름/신문광고/인터넷 주소 등등)

- 왜 그 자리에 지원하는지를 열정/의지를 담아서 표현합니다.
  - 하지만 간단명료하게 적습니다.

2) Cover Letter 본분(Body)에 포함되어야 할 내용

- 첫 번째 문단(구태의연한 인사 문장은 필요치 않습니다!)
  1. 반드시 응모하는 회사 또는 호텔/레스토랑의 좋은 점을 명시합니다.
  2. 응모동기, 즉 어떻게 응모하게 되었는지를 반드시 기재합니다(지인/신문광고/방송/인터넷 등). 만약, 광고를 통해서가 아니고 빈자리가 없을 경우에 지원하는 것이라면 "possible opening"(혹시 있을지도 모르는 기회)이라고 적습니다.
  3. 항상 응모하는 회사의 명칭을 확실하게 명시합니다. (줄이거나 귀사라고 쓰지 않습니다.)

- 두 번째 문단(가장 중요한 부분)
  1. 꼭 이 회사에서 일하고 싶은 열정을 보여주어야 합니다.
  2. 왜 당신이 이 회사에 꼭 필요한 존재인지 간단하지만 확실한 존재감을 보여주는 문장이 필요합니다.
  3. 가능하면, 지난번 직장에서 했던 일을 긍정적으로 언급합니다. 어떤 참신한 아이디어와 혁신적인 일을 하였는가? 그리고 그 결과는 어떠했는가?
- 세 번째 문단
  1. 이 회사/레스토랑에서 꼭 일하게 되면 좋겠다는 당신의 의지/열정을 표현합니다.
  2. 인사 담당자를 만나서 면접 보고 싶다고 적극적으로 말합니다.
  3. 정중하지만 본인이 이 회사에 반드시 귀한 재산이 될 것임을 각인시킵니다.

이제 다음 Cover Letter Template를 보고 본인 것을 작성해 봅시다.

Cover Letter Template (커버레터 틀)

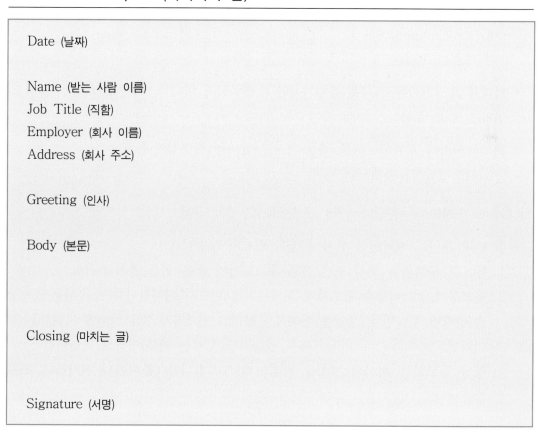

Date (날짜)

Name (받는 사람 이름)
Job Title (직함)
Employer (회사 이름)
Address (회사 주소)

Greeting (인사)

Body (본문)

Closing (마치는 글)

Signature (서명)

아래 3종류의 샘플 Cover Letter를 참고해서 본인 것을 작성해 봅시다.

Sample 1
Cover Letter for Hotel or Kitchen Staff(학생용)

May 25, 20XX

Mr. James Brown
Human Resources Manager,
ABC Hotel,
123 ○○○-ro gil, Jung-gu,
Seoul, Korea

Dear Mr. Brown,

I'm responding to your recent advertisement of the Second Cook Position in the ABC Hotel in Seoul on your web site. I am well qualified for the position in your Hotel and I know that I could make a significant contribution to your hotel.

Although I have enclosed my resume, let me quickly highlight some of my relevant experiences. Through my in-depth on-the-job-training at the xxx Hotel, I had hands-on experience in Italian kitchen for two months. I also worked at a local Italian restaurant as an assistant cook for 4 months. I understand how a western restaurant works in a hotel, I learn quickly, and I am comfortable working as a cooking team under time pressure.

I hope that we will be able to meet in person to discuss the Second Cook position in the hotel. I am looking forward to speaking with you soon.

Sincerely,

(타이핑한 이름 위에 <u>반드시</u> 검은색으로 자필 사인할 것!)
Hong, Gil-dong
Cell Phone: 010-1234-5678

March 2, 20XX (날짜)

Mr. John Doe (받는 사람 성명과 주소)
1234 Abc Rd.,
Los Angles, CA, 34567

Dear Sir,

I am interested in pursuing a career in the hotel and restaurant service industry. I am a new graduate from the University of XXXX under its Hotel and Culinary Program. I have received basic kitchen training for three months as an apprentice and kitchen steward at Sushi Max. This internship has allowed me to learn from experienced sushi chefs their various food preparation techniques in handling raw fish meat. The experience has also provided me the opportunity to work under a team under strict guidelines and time limits set by the master chef.

I guarantee you that I am a very passionate and positive individual who dreams to become an experience and well-rounded chef someday.

I would appreciate the opportunity to discuss my skills with you and find out more about your job requirements. I am also open to any training opportunities as a contractual kitchen staff. I am returning to the city from Spring break after April 8. Would it be possible to meet then?

Sincerely,

(Signature - 본인 서명)
Hankook Kim (이름 타이핑해서 입력할 것)

Sample 3
Cover Letter(경력자용)

April 3, 20XX

Mr. Jetson Horton
Buckshots Steak and Seafood
108 North Thomas Ave.
Sayre, PA

Dear Mr. Horton,

After having seen and heard numerous good reviews about the food and service at Buckshots, I decided to apply for the position Sous Chef as seen in Binghamton Press & Sun Bulletin.

I am very eager to be considered for the position, and believe that I have the qualifications and skills needed to be a top candidate. Having worked for many years as the Assistant Chef at historic O'Brien's Inn I am willing and able to step up to the next level. I have created new recipes and combinations that were well received by the guests of the Inn, with this causing average ticket receipts to increase by 30% over a 4-year period. I also have the ability to learn menu items quickly and well.

I would consider it an honor and privilege to work with you at Buckshots Steak and Seafood and hope I am granted an opportunity to meet or talk with you in the very near future.

Sincerely,

(Signature - 본인 서명할 것)
Alice G. Parry

2. 영문 이력서 작성법

해외에서 인턴이나 취업을 하고 싶은 경우, 회사가 정해준 서식이 있으면 서식에 맞게 응시자의 경험이나 경력, 자격조건 등을 작성하면 됩니다. 하지만 특별한 양식이 없다면, 아래의 설명을 자세히 읽어본 후에 본인의 경력, 학력에 맞게 준비해 봅시다.

영문 이력서는 예전에 'Personal History' 또는 'Curriculum Vitae'라고 했지만 요즘에는 보통 Resume(레주메 : 불어식 발음)라고 합니다. 이 Resume 작성법은 한글 이력서와 유사한 내용들이 포함되지만 작성방법이 다릅니다.

먼저, 영문 이력서에는 기본적으로 간단한 개인정보(이름/주소/전화번호)와 경력을 "최근 순서"로 기재하여야 합니다.

우리나라는 본인의 개인정보는 물론 학력, 경력, 출신 배경 등을 오래된 순서대로 나열하고 서술하는 데 반해, 영문 이력서는 간단한 신상정보, 경력목표, 지난 업적들을 명확하게 표현합니다(가능한 수치화해서 적습니다). 또한, 중요한 포인트는 한글 이력서와는 정반대로 가장 최근에 일어난 일부터 순서대로 서술한다는 점입니다. 그래서 현재하고 있는 일 → 그전에 다녔던 직장 → 등등의 순서로 열거한다는 점에 유의해야 합니다. 이것은 반드시 명심하고 지켜야 하는 부분입니다.

그리고 미국에서는 이력서에 사진을 첨부하지 않습니다. 놀라운 사실이죠? 그 이유는 미국의 'Equal Right Opportunity'에 어긋나기 때문입니다. 하지만 한국에 있는 외국회사에 지원할 경우 Resume 상단에 사진을 첨부하는 것이 한국정서에 적절하겠지요. 만약 확신이 없다면 지원하는 회사에 전화해서 알아보시는 것이 확실한 방법이 될 수 있습니다.

영문 이력서를 작성하는 형식을 표로 나타내면 다음과 같습니다.

Personal Information
개인정보
(이름/주소/전화번호/E-mail 주소)

·

·

Career Objective
경력목표

·

·

Work Experience
경력 및 업적
(경력은 최근 순서로 적고, 업적은 가능한 한 수치로 표시한다)

·

·

Education
학력
(학력도 가징 최근에 다녔던 학교부터 열거하고 초등학교는 생략해도 좋다)

Awards
수상경력
(수상한 경력도 최근 순서로 적는다)

·

Certificates or License
자격증 또는 면허증
(이 부분도 반드시 가장 최근 순서로 적는 것임을 명심할 것)

·

Personals
추가적인 개인정보
(외국어 능력/운전면허증/취미 등을 필요할 때만 기재한다)

〈주의사항!〉

영문 이력서는 반드시 모든 부분을 "최근 순서"로 기재한다는 것을 반드시 명심하고 그대로 지켜야 한다.

대부분의 외국계 회사는 국내 기업의 문화와는 달리 개인의 신상, 가족관계 등은 중요하게 생각하지 않고, 현재 입사지원한 사람의 능력을 최대한 판단하기 위한 도구로 이력서를 확인하기 때문에 이 점을 꼭 염두에 두고 자신을 가장 잘 PR할 수 있는 내용으로 영문 이력서를 작성해야 합니다.

1) 구체적인 영문 이력서 작성 순서

자, 이제 구체적으로 영문 이력서를 어떻게 작성하는지 알아보고 적어보는 연습을 해봅시다.

① Personal Information(간단한 개인정보)

인사 담당자가 꼭 알아야 하는 본인의 간단한 개인정보(이름/주소/전화번호)만 기재합니다. - 국내 기업처럼 많은 정보(가족구성원, 혈액형, 종교, 시력 등)를 적을 필요는 없습니다.

② 일반적으로 본인의 이름(First Name), 성(Last Name 또는 Family Name)의 순서로 씁니다.

예 : Hankook Kim

또한, 한국 스타일로 성을 먼저 써도 됩니다. 하지만 이 경우에는 성(Last Name)을 먼저 썼다는 표시를 반드시 해야 합니다. 본인의 성 다음에 ",(쉼표)" 표시를 하면 됩니다.

예 : Kim, Hankook

③ Career Objective

아무런 목표가 없이 "그냥 이런 사람이 되는 것이 목표입니다."라고 할 경우 현실성이 없다고 판단되어 마이너스가 될 수 있습니다. 나의 목표가 무엇인지 정확하고 명료하게 적어주는 것이 좋습니다. 예를 들어 "Executive Chef가 되고 싶다", 또는 "Sous Chef가 되고 싶다"라고 구체적으로 적는 것이 바람직합니다.

④ Job Experience

외국계 기업은 국내 기업처럼 출신 학교보다는 개인의 능력을 중시합니다. 내가 어떤 경험을 가지고 어떤 것을 잘할 수 있는지에 초점을 맞추어서 정리하여 자신의 장점을 극대화하여 작성하는 것이 좋습니다.

⑤ Educational Background

앞에서 언급하였듯이 학력도 우리의 전통적인 생각의 역순으로 적습니다. 다시 말해서 제일 최근에 졸업한 학력부터 간단히 적습니다(학교이름/학위명/전공과 명칭). 초등학교, 중등학교는 쓰지 않아도 됩니다.

◆ 영문 이력서 작성 10계명

앞에서 언급된 내용을 다시 한 번 간단하게 요약하면 아래와 같습니다.

① 커버레터(Cover Letter)로 자신을 PR하라

인사 담당자의 경우 커버레터를 읽은 후 이력서를 읽을지 여부를 판단하기 때문에 자신을 최대한 PR하는 것이 좋습니다.

② 현실성 있는 비전을 제시하라

영어 실력이 다소 부족하여도 전문적인 능력을 갖추고 있고 자신만의 꿈이 있다고 자신감을 피력하는 것이 좋습니다. 만약 자신감 있는 비전을 제시하지 못한다면 당연히 탈락의 고배를 마실 것입니다.

③ 능력과 경력에 초점을 맞춰라

외국계 기업은 개인의 능력에 초점을 맞추어서 사람을 뽑습니다. 짧은 아르바이트 경력이라도 해당 기업과 관련이 있는 업종 혹은 교육을 받았다면 모두 기재하여 자신을 PR하는 것이 좋습니다.

④ 자신만의 색깔을 찾아라

외국계 기업은 모범적인 사람보다 창의적이고 도전적인 인재를 선호하는 편입니다. 이력 중 남들과 다른 이력이 있다면 주저하지 마시고 적어주는 것이 좋습니다.

⑤ 사소한 것까지 신경 써라

외국계 기업은 자신을 철저하게 관리하는 인재를 선호합니다. 이력서 작성 시에도 페이지 번호 및 이력사항 연결에 대한 힌트 등을 꼼꼼하게 적어주는 것이 좋습니다.

⑥ 지원동기 및 분야를 분명히 밝혀라

외국계 기업에서는 정확한 지원 분야를 밝히지 않을 경우 자신만의 전문 분야가 없다고 판단하여 탈락의 고배를 마실 수 있으니 정확한 지원동기 및 분야를 적는 것이 좋습니다.

⑦ 지원하는 회사와 업무에 맞춰 작성하라

외국계 기업은 즉각적으로 현장에 투입할 수 있는 인재를 원합니다. 이력서 작성 시에도 해당 업무를 이미 담당할 수 있는 능력이 있다는 것을 입증하는 것이 중요합니다.

⑧ 공백기간 동안의 실적을 밝혀라

경력상 공백기간은 있을 수 있습니다. 공백기간 동안 무엇을 준비했는지 명확하게 적어주는 것이 좋습니다.

⑨ 경력자는 구체적인 수치를 통해 실적을 설명하라

자신의 능력을 입증할 수 있는 근거 자료를 준비해서 보여주세요. 지속적으로 언급하고 있지만 외국계 기업은 개인의 역량을 가장 중요시합니다. 수치화할 수 없는 데이터보다는 수치화하여 보여줄 수 있는 데이터를 하나라도 더 보여주는 것이 좋습니다.

⑩ 한국의 실정을 반영하라

외국계 기업이지만 국내에 있다면 한국인이 인사 담당자가 될 수 있으니 기본적인 인적 사항들은 기록해 주는 것이 좋습니다.

2) Cover Letter와 영문 이력서 체크리스트 7가지

① 정직하게 : 아무런 거짓 없이 학력 및 경력 기재
② 명확하게 : 지금까지 한 일과 쌓아온 경험을 명확하게
③ 단정하게 : 디자인은 깔끔하고 매끄럽게
④ 한눈에 들어오게 : 다 똑같은 형식보다는 조금 더 정확한 내용으로 작성
  (오랜 경력자 외에는 한 페이지에 모든 정보를 기록하는 것이 좋습니다.)
⑤ 내용은 충실하게 : 수치화할 수 있는 내용은 명확하게 적어서 작성
⑥ 맞춤식으로 : 회사가 요구하는 형식에 맞게 잘 파악해서 작성
⑦ 알파의 여력 : 남들과 다른 나만의 경쟁력은 무엇인지 작성

〈반드시 피해야 할 사항들〉
1. 외국계 회사의 경우 한국과 문화의 차이 때문에 한국과 같은 형식으로 이력서를 제출할 경우에는 100% 서류 전형에 낙오할 것이니 꼭 기억해 둡니다.
2. 불분명한 목표를 제시하지 않습니다.
3. 이력서에 허위 내용을 기재하지 않습니다.

〈주의사항〉
Cover Letter가 Resume 위에 오도록 하는 것 잊지 않으셨죠?

3) Resume Template(영문 이력서 틀)

Name
Street Address
E-mail Address
Cell-Phone Number ── (크고 간결하게 한눈에 들어오게 기재한다.)

Career Objective (1-2줄로 간단히 적기)

Experience (최근 순서로 적기 - 번호는 붙이지 않는다)

Education (최근 순서로 학력 적기 - 간단히 전공과목과 학교이름을 적는다)

Awards (수상기록을 최근 순서로 기록한다)

Certificates (자격증 등을 최근 순서로 기록한다)

Personal (외국어 구사 능력 등을 최근 순서로 기재한다)

Hong, Gil-dong

123-4567 ABC Apt., ○○○-ro gil, Mapo-gu, Seoul, S. Korea
Cell Phone: 010-1234-5678
E-mail : honggildong@naver.com

Objective:

Seeking a challenging entry level cook position in a leading hotel restaurant where I can pursue my enthusiasm for western culinary arts

Experience:

9, 2013 – Present : Currently working part-time at an Italian restaurant "La Cucina" as an assistant cook
7, 2013 – 8, 2013 : Worked at the Cold Kitchen in the Lotte Hotel in Seoul as a "on-the-job trainee"
12, 2012 – 2, 2013 : Worked at the "Mr. Pizza" in Daegu as a delivery person

Education:

3, 2010 – Present : Currently attending the Dept. of Western Culinary Arts of the Daegu Health College, Daegu
3, 2007 – 2, 2010 : Graduated from the ABC High School, Seoul
3, 2004 – 2, 2007 : Graduated from the DEF Middle School, Busan

Awards:

6, 2013   : Awarded the First Prize at the "5th College Student Cooking Contest" in Seoul
9, 2013   : Awarded the Third Prize at the "Daegu Cooking Contest" in Seoul

Certificates:

5, 2013   : Obtained a certificate of Western Cuisine
4, 2013   : Obtained a certificate of Korean Cuisine

Personal:

12, 2010 – 1, 2012 : Completed Military Service in ROK Army
6, 2011   : Obtained a Driver's License

(＊ "ROK"은 'Republic of Korea'의 약자이며 뜻은 '대한민국'이다.)

Hankook Kim,

101-101 Hankook Apt.,
○○○-ro gil, Gangnam-gu,
Seoul, S. Korea
Cell Phone : (010)-XXX-XXXX

Objective : Seeking for a position of cook for a leading restaurant where I can prove myself with better service.

Work Experience :
City Babes Cafe, Royal Oak
Executive Cook

Responsibilities :
- Prepared restaurant items such as wraps, sandwiches, salads, pizza, pasta etc.
- Carry out duties of recording and order control.
- Some custom designed menus were also created for special and private clients.
- Managed all duties and trained to new employees.
- Also prepared promotional and marketing materials.
- Responsible for various other duties as assigned and as needed.

Collins Hotels Inc., Tarrytown, NY
Worked as Assistant Cook
- Responsible for helping in food control and inventory.
- Responsible for helping in the preparation and serving the meal.
- Organized constant cleaning of kitchen and dining room.
- Make sure about the cleanness and safety of floors.
- Responsible for helping in cleaning and keeping the camp neat.
- Make simple food items such as sandwiches, brewing coffee and carving meats.

Education :
Diploma in Hotel Management, New York University, NY

AMY SMITH

123 Main Street, Atlanta, Georgia, 30339

Home : (555) 555-1234, Cell : (555) 555-1235

asmith@sample~resume.com

Objective : Seek the Position of Sous Chef

SUMMARY : Profoundly creative, innovative and self motivated Sous Chef with huge background assisting management of Casino food service department; monitoring employee performance, preparing schedules, overseeing menu and food preparation and insuring excellent customer service.

Summary of Qualifications

- Ten years experience.
- Exceptional knowledge of 24 hour, seven day a week food and beverage operation.
- Strong ability to communicate effectively to all levels of staff.
- Sound up to date knowledge of Food Safety Guidelines, First Aid/C.P.R.
- Environmental Health codes, Local, State and Federal Guidelines.
- Excellent organizational and communication skills.
- Uncommon skill in all technical and sanitary aspects of food preparation and presentations.
- Remarkable ability to stand for long lengths of time.
- In-depth ability to lift up to 50 pounds of product.

Professional Experience

Galaxy Casino Inc., Minneapolis

2002 - Present

Sous Chef

Responsible for supervision of the entire kitchen operation under the direction of Executive Chef.

Review with Executive Chef all scheduling of kitchen employees.

Assist the Chef in all aspects of hiring, training, review, and termination of kitchen employees.

Maintain and update all required files and company documentation forms.

With the Executive Chef, review food and labor costs of entire operation on a regular basis.

Follow all applicable State, Federal, Tribal and Local Laws, and Policies and Procedures established by the Casino.

Perform all assigned tasks essential to 24-hour casino operations.

Accept responsibility for compliance with rules and regulations, and for own decisions and those of subordinates.

Effectively develop individual, departmental, and organizational goals to meet objectives of the Casino.

Determine the needs of the assigned departments, specify procedures and administer written policies.

Achieve optimal performance and accomplishment from assigned kitchen staff.

Galaxy Hotel Inc., Rainbow County, Minneapolis
2000 - 2002

Lead Line Cook

Ensured quality and quantity of foodstuffs according to standards and specifications as determined by the Restaurant Chef.

Cooked and prepared food according to recipes.

Cut, trimmed and boned meats and poultry for cooking.

Portioned cooked foods according to size of portions and methods of garnishing.

Cleaned and sanitized equipment used.

Provided support to Chef and production leadership to subordinates.

Prepared and maintained the station used for prep cooks.

Maintained sanitary working environment at all times.

Responsible for following resort recipes and ensured Galaxy quality of meals for guests.

Responsible for promoting positive morale in kitchen.

Assisted Sous Chef in the creation of specials, soups etc.

Galaxy Hotel Inc., Rainbow County, Minneapolis
1997 – 2000

Cook

Prepared and cooked meats, vegetables, and casserole dishes for general and modified diet menus using hand and power kitchen utensils and equipment.

Prepared foods for persons on specialized diets (i.e., diabetic, salt restricted, religious) and modified texture diets (i.e., pureed, ground). Reconstituted and heated convenience food; heated, steamed, and baked frozen and canned food. Prepared salads, desserts, and beverages.

Prepared food for special occasions such as meetings, birthdays, and holiday celebrations.

Assembled food for transportation, as required, by measuring out food, placing in proper containers, and loading hot and cold food carts; received and unloaded returned carts; disposed of unused food; and removed soiled ware for washing.

Participated in, and guided others, in the washing, sanitizing, and cleaning of the premises, cooking utensils, and kitchen equipment such as pots and pans, steam kettles, automatic slicers, choppers, blenders, refrigerators, ovens, freezers, microwaves, tables, and carts to maintain sanitary conditions.

Inspected food and food products prior to use and consumption for quality and freedom from contamination and spoilage; rotated stored food stock to ensure proper and timely usage.

Received and put away stock such as canned goods, paper products, fish, meats, cereal, flour, sugar, and eggs; maintained inventory and orders food items as necessary.

Education

Associate Degree in Dietetics
University of New York (1997)

Sample 4(회사에서 요구하는 특정한 이력서 양식이 있는 경우)

증명사진
셀프 카메라 가능

반드시 워드로 작성 **Times new roman**체, 글자크기 12pt

Name : (반드시 여권 이름과 동일하게 기재)

    (이름)   (성)

Address : (포털사이트에서 영문주소 찾아 기재 ; 호, 번지, 동, 구, 시, 국가 순)

Telephone/Mobile No : 82-32-277-4700 / 82-10-293-1111

        (국가번호 82, 지역번호 0 빼고 기재)

E-mail : (hanmail은 빼고 기재)

Position applied : **Culinary Arts** (희망부서)

PERSONAL DETAILS

Date of Birth : **6, March 1980**(생년월일 기재)

Nationality : **Republic of Korea** (국적; 대한민국)

Sex(성별) : Male(남자) / Female(여자) **Marital Status** : **Single** (결혼여부)

Birth City : **Seoul** (태어난 도시명)

You Tube Video Link : (유튜브 링크 주소 : 동영상 만드는 방법 및 올리는 첨부자료 참고)

OBJECTIVE *인턴십에 참여한 목적 / 목표*

Aiming to acquire the necessary skills, abilities and experience that will help me become a manager of a hotel or resort when I return to my home country.

EDUCATION *교육*

Mar. 2010~Present　University of Korea(대학교명)　Seoul, Korea(지역, 국가)

*입학연도　* 2년제는 Diploma / 3년제는 Advanced Diploma

　　　　　　4년제는 Bachelor 꼭 적기*

Major : *학과 전공*

Courses Taken (현재 영어 성적표 그대로 기재**)**

Food	Science	
Culinary	Skill Development	
Nutrition		
Food	Safety	
Introduction	to Gastronomy	
Meat	Seafood Identification	
	and Fabrication	
Bread	Baking	
Introduction	of Hot Foods	
Menu and	Cuisine Management	
Management	of Wine	
Introduction	of Cold Foods	
Patisserie		

EXPERIENCE (경력**)　Total Work Experience : 18 months (**전체 경력기간**)**

(최근 경력부터 작성, 단기아르바이트 / 취사병 등 모든 경력 포함 가능)

Feb. 2010~Jun. 2011

Sheraton hotel *(회사명)*   **Seoul, Korea** *(지역, 국가)*

Position : cook

(구체적으로 했던 업무)

- Assisted a Chef
- Prepared cooking, Trimmed vegetables
- Line cooking, preparing, assisting chef with ordering

Supervisor Name and Title : Kim, hong gil / Executive Chef (책임자 이름 / 직위)

82-2-123-1234 *연락처*

- **Date would like to start** : July, 2011 (출국 희망날짜)

EXTRA CURRICULAR ACTIVITIES

(교내활동 및 동아리 / 봉사활동)

Mar. 2012 Voluntary reading service for visually handicapped people

CERTIFICATE OF QUALIFICATION

(자격증)

Oct. 2012 The certificate in professional Western food.

HONORS AND AWARDS (대회 참가 경험 및 수상 경력을 적어주세요)

- Awarded scholarship given to top 3% of class in 2002, 2003, 2006 Hankook University
- Awarded best Army prize in 2006 Korea Army

4) 영문 추천서

① 영문 추천서 References

영문 추천서 제출이유 : 일반적으로 저희 인턴십 프로그램의 참가자일 경우 경력사항 등이 적으므로 인턴십 관계자가 우수한 인력인지 그리고 어떠한 인력인지를 판단하기가 힘듭니다. 그리고 인턴십 관계자뿐만 아니라 DS-2019 스폰서 기관에도 참가자에게 신뢰성을 주기 위하여 이 추천서가 필요합니다.

<u>영문 추천서 유의사항</u>

- 추천인 2명이 필요하며 각 1명에게서 동일한 추천서 2장씩을 받습니다. 즉 추천인이 2명이면 4장의 추천서가 됩니다. 1명에게서 2장을 받는 경우는 인턴십 관계자 및 DS-2019 스폰서 기관 2곳에 사용되기 때문입니다.

- 추천인의 명함이 필요합니다. 미국이라서 추천서의 직접적인 확인이 힘들기 때문에 명함 또한 추천인으로부터 2장씩 받습니다.

- 대학교수에게서 추천서를 받을 경우 학교 공식 레터지(서식)에 추천서를 받습니다. 학교 레터지는 대학에서 공식적으로 대내외에 사용하는 용지로써 학교 로고와 주소 등이 용지에 인쇄되어 있습니다. 취업보도실이나 학과사무실, 학교서무실 등지에 배치되어 있습니다.

- 회사의 책임자에게 받는 경우에도 가능한 회사로고가 있는 용지에 받는 것이 좋으며, 없으면 일반용지에 받아옵니다.

- 일반적으로 교수님 등 추천인 등이 영문 추천서를 쓴 경험이 적으므로 다음과 같은 방법을 사용하기도 합니다. 참가자 본인이 레터지 등을 구해서 추천서 내용을 모두 기재한 후 추천인의 서명과 명함만 받아옵니다. 그러나 이때도 반드시 추천서의 내용과 인턴십의 참가목적 등을 고지하여야 합니다.

② 추천인의 자격

일반적으로 경력자라면 이전 근무처의 상사나 대학의 지도교수 등의 연락처를 쓰면 되고 별도의 양식은 없습니다. 졸업예정자의 경우는 지도교수나 선배, 프로젝트 수행경험 시 책임자급으로 하면 무난합니다. 신원보증인이라기보다는 본인의 능력이나 자질에 대해 보증할 수 있는 제3자를 말하며, 부모 형제나 친척은 해당되지 않습니다.

- 대학 학과 교수 및 인턴십 관련학과 교수
- 사설교육기관 강사 및 원장
- 인턴십 관련회사의 과장급 이상 인사(호텔 매니저 등)
- 관련 공공기관의 인사 및 사회적 저명인사

③ 영문 추천서 기재내용

- 추천인의 성명, 소속기관, 소속직위, 주소, 전화
- 추천인과 인턴십 지원자와의 관계를 서술
- 인턴십과 관련하여 참가자가 인턴십을 수행하는 데 충분한 자격이 있다는 내용(필수)
- 인턴십의 참가결과가 참가자에게 많은 도움이 될 것이라는 내용(필수)
- 인턴십 수료 후 반드시 한국으로 귀국할 것이라는 내용(필수)

④ 참가자 개인평가사항

- 어학능력 : 인턴십을 수행하기 위하여 충분하다는 평가
- 교육관계 : 참가자가 이수한 과목 등은 인턴십을 수행할 수 있는 충분한 사전지식이 된다는 평가
- 경력상황 : 참가자의 경력이 인턴십을 수행할 수 있는 충분한 경력이 된다는 평가
- 대인관계(지도성·협동성·사려성)
  참가자가 동료들의 생각과 마음을 합하여 어떤 좋은 방향으로 끌고 간 경우, 공동체의 구성원으로서 개인적인 태도를 취하지 않고 적극적으로 행동한 경우, 다양한 친구들을 사귀며 친밀하게 지낸 경우, 친구의 고민을 상담해 주고 도움을 준 경우 등
- 봉사정신과 봉사활동
  주변의 어려운 사람들을 돕기 위해 자신의 시간과 노력을 아끼지 않은 경우, 공동체를 위해 다른 사람들이 꺼리는 일에 자원하여 봉사한 경우 등
- 내적 성숙성 및 생활태도(정직성·책임성·성실성)
  바람직한 가치기준에 따라 상황을 판단하고 용기 있게 행동한 경우, 자신에게 부여된 일을 완수하기 위해 최선을 다한 경우, 자신의 목표를 이루기 위해 계획적으로 생활한 경우 등

5) 영문 추천서 Sample

June 10, 20XX

To Whom It May Concern :

Dear Sir/Ma'am,

I am so pleased to write this reference letter for Ms. Kilja, Hong. I have taught her since 20XX and I am very familiar with her. She was one of the most promising and outstanding students I have taught.

During this past 3 years, she has been a good student and got good grades. She was diligent and very quick to pick things up and developed herself through various tasks and performance.

The most remarkable activities, as far as I remember, came from her dignity and passion during performing her project. She conducted market research as a team leader, designed a program to test its validity and finally verified her thesis was right. To set aside the truth of her program, I was very impressed by her enthusiasm and concentration. Also she was warm and kind, so it was easy to make friends with her. Many times she was observed to get along with her peer group.

If you give her opportunity to participate to your internship program, your organization can benefit her dignity and honesty.

Without reservation, I strongly recommend Ms Kilja, Hong to your internship program and if you have any question about her please feel free to contact me to 82-2-6000-2000.

Sincerely,

Kim, ○○
Professor of ○○○ University

Chapter 2

영어 면접

1. Expected Interview Questions(예상 면접질문)

아래 내용들은 영어로 면접 볼 때 자주 나오는 질문을 간추려본 것이다. 이런 질문들이 나올 때 당황하지 말고 차분히 대답할 수 있도록 차근차근 준비해 보자.

1. Why do you want to take part in the H2b/J1 program at ABC?
   왜 ABC의 H2b/J1 프로그램에 참여하시려고 하십니까?

2. Why do you want to work for ABC's?
   왜 ABC에서 일하려고 하나요?

3. Tell me about yourself.
   본인 소개를 해주세요.

4. Do you have any working experience, have you worked with the public / customer service?
   전에 일한 경력이 있나요? 고객 응대 서비스 쪽 일을 해보신 적이 있나요?

5. Tell me about some experiences you might have had serving customers in a previous job.
   전에 하신 일 중에서 고객 서비스를 해보신 경험이 있으면 말해 주세요.

6. What do you consider good customer service?
   좋은 고객 서비스란 무엇이라고 생각하십니까?

7. What are your best qualities as a worker?
   당신이 지닌 자질 중에서 가장 좋은 것은 무엇인가요?

8. Give me three words that best describe your personality at work.
   당신이 일할 때 당신의 성품을 나타내는 가장 좋은 3가지 단어는 무엇인가요?

9. Think about your prior supervisors (or teachers if you do not have job experience), how would they describe you?
   당신의 전 직장 상사(또는 선생님)가 당신을 어떻게 묘사할까요?

10. What motivates you in a work environment?

직장에서 당신은 무엇으로 동기부여를 받나요?

11. What did you like most about your previous job?

전 직장에서 가장 좋았던 점은 무엇인가요?

12. Where do you see yourself ten years from now?

10년 후에 당신은 무엇을 하고 있을까요?

13. Tell me about a past experience in which you had to utilize supervisory skill in a job performance or school related function.

직장이나 학교에서 당신은 어떤 지도자의 능력을 사용했는지 말해 주세요.

14. In your opinion, what is the best trait that should be maintained as a supervisor?

지도자(직장 상사)란 어떤 덕목을 지녀야 한다고 생각하십니까?

15. Describe how your experience, abilities, and knowledge best qualify you for this position.

당신의 어떤 지난 경력이나 지식이나 능력이 이 직업에 자격이 있다고 생각하십니까?

16. What is your greatest achievement?

당신의 가장 큰 업적은 무엇입니까?

17. How would you go about establishing your credibility quickly with the company? And fellow co-workers?

당신은 어떻게 회사에서 그리고 동료 사이에서 당신의 신뢰성을 인식시키시겠습니까?

18. What's the most important thing you learned in school?

학교에서 배운 가장 중요한 것은 무엇입니까?

2. 예상 면접 질문과 답변(Interview Questions and Answers)

Situation

For a job interview, job applicants need to be familiar with a number of things to be employed by the hotel/restaurants you are applying for. They include its corporate philosophy, managerial policies, commitment to the community, corporate scale, places of business, and corporate indemnity system. You also need to think about what you can do for the hotel/restaurant when you are employed. Once you are hired, you need to work on shifts and get ready for board and lodging. You should be aware of these things and be able to answer the questions related to these issues when you have a job interview. Possible job interview questions and answers are presented here to help you prepare it.

상황

취업을 앞두고, 예비 직장인이 준비해야 할 것들은 매우 많다. 우선 그 호텔이나 레스토랑이 지향하는 기업의 철학, 경영방향, 사회기여도, 규모, 업장의 종류, 종업원 보상제도 등 많은 것을 익혀야 한다. 뿐만 아니라 당해 호텔이나 레스토랑이 지원자를 고용할 경우 그 회사를 위해 어떠한 기여를 할 수 있는지도 매우 중요한 요인이 된다. 또한 고용이 되면 주5일간 불규칙적으로 출퇴근해야 하므로 숙식문제도 대두된다. 이러한 것들을 계획적으로 준비하고, 면접에 응하면 면접에 성공할 확률이 매우 높아진다. 다음의 내용은 인터뷰 실전에 활용되는 Q&A이다.

꼼꼼하게 잘 읽어보고 본인에게 맞도록 수정하여 미리미리 연습한다면 어떤 면접에서도 자신있게 대처할 수 있을 것이다.

Q Can you tell me about yourself.
본인에 대해 말해 보십시오.

A I am graduating from ABC College(or University) and majored in culinary. Being a chef has been my dream for a long time. I'm easy going and calm. I'm reliable, friendly, capable, and honest.

저의 이력서에서 보시다시피 저는 호텔조리학을 전공하고 ABC 대학교를 졸업할 예정입니다. 주방장이 되는 것이 나의 오랜 꿈이었습니다. 저는 소탈하고 차분한 성격입니다. 신뢰할 만하고 친근하며, 능력이 있고 정직합니다.

As you can see from my resume, I'm working part-time on weekends at the ○○Hotel but I have also worked at a number of different part-time jobs in the service industry. My most interesting job so far was at the Lotte Hotel where I helped with the organization of their food and beverage operations. I enjoyed this work especially because it required a lot of attention to the guests and fellow employees.

저의 이력서를 보셨듯이, 저는 ○○호텔에서 주말 파트타임으로 일하고 있습니다. 뿐만 아니라 시간이 되면 다른 서비스업종에서도 파트타임 일을 하고 있습니다. 저는 지금 서비스하고 있는 ○○호텔 식음료부서에서 일하는 데 가장 큰 흥미를 느낍니다. 저는 이 일이 고객과 동료 종업원들에게 항상 신경을 쓰게 되어, 이를 즐기고 있습니다.

Q What was the subject that you enjoyed most at school?
대학에서 가장 흥미로웠던 과목은 무엇입니까?

A I like foreign languages the best. I like Japanese. I thought the ability to speak other languages would be a great asset to me as a hotelier when I work for people from all over the world.

외국어 공부를 좋아합니다. 일본어를 좋아합니다. 외국어를 말할 수 있는 능력이 세계 여러 곳에서 온 손님들을 위해 일할 때 도움이 될 것이라는 생각을 했습니다.

Q How would you describe your strengths?
본인의 장점에 대해 말해 주십시오.

A I pay attention to details and I'm patient. I'm very thorough and I work well with a team. I have a good sense of humor and I've been told that I put guests at ease. My ability to work with all types of people is one of my greatest strengths. I enjoy learning and improving my knowledge. It takes up much of my spare time, though.

저는 꼼꼼하고 인내심이 강합니다. 저는 완벽한 것을 좋아하고 팀의 일원으로 같이 일하는 것을 잘합니다. 저는 유머감각이 좋고 제가 보통 손님을 편하게 해드린다고들 합니다. 어떤 종류의 사람들과도 잘 어울려 일하는 것이 나의 장점입니다.

장점이면서 단점이라고도 할 수 있는데 새로운 것을 배우는 것을 좋아해서 여유 시간을 잘 즐기지 못합니다.

Q What is your greatest strength?
당신의 가장 큰 장점은 무엇입니까?

A (답변 예1)
I'm easy going and I think I make friends very easily. Wherever I travel I like to meet new people and I keep in touch with them. At my last birthday party there were more than 50 friends in my house.

저는 친구를 매우 쉽게 사귄다고 생각합니다. 제가 어디에 가든 주변에 사람이 많고, 한번 만난 사람들과는 좋은 교류를 해오고 있습니다. 지난번 저의 생일 땐 50명이 넘는 친구들이 저희 집에 와서 축하를 해주었습니다.

(답변 예2 : 위와 같은 질문의 조금 다른 답변)
Well, my greatest strength is my ability to get to know people. I love to meet new people. I seem to be able to make people feel comfortable right away. Maybe it's because I really enjoy listening to them.

저의 장점은 사람을 잘 사귀는 것이라고 말씀드립니다. 저는 새로운 사람을 만나는 것을 아주 좋아합니다. 저는 사람을 만나면 곧바로 편안하게 해줍니다. 아마 그것은 말하기보다 듣기를 좋아하는 게 원인인 것 같습니다.

Q What is your greatest weakness?

당신의 가장 큰 단점은 무엇입니까?

A I enjoy talking to people and I know that in the past I spent too much time on the telephone. Now I watch the clock while I'm making business calls and I've cut my telephone time in half.

저는 사람들과 대화하는 것을 좋아하여 많은 시간을 전화하면서 보내곤 했습니다. 그러나 이젠 사업상 전화라도 시간 관리를 위해 시계를 보면서 통화를 하게 되므로 시간을 반으로 줄일 수 있었습니다.

Q What kind of weaknesses do you have?

당신의 단점은 무엇입니까?

A I'm a perfectionist so I sometimes stay back at work to check if everything is OK. I need to improve my skills in English grammar, so I'm continuing my studies.

저는 완벽주의자여서 모든 것이 완벽하게 될 때까지 남아서 일하기도 하는데 때때로 이런 성격이 저의 문제점입니다.

저는 영어문법실력을 더 향상시켜야 합니다. 그래서 매주 공부하고 있습니다.

Q Why should we hire you?

왜 우리가 당신을 고용해야 합니까?

A I have been trained for the hospitality business and am interested in the culinary area. I took an internship training program in your hotel. I believe I am ready and fit for the job. It's been my dream to work in your hotel ever since I decided to become a hotelier.

저는 환대산업분야에서 훈련을 받았고 특히 조리 분야에 관심이 많습니다. 이 호텔에서 인턴십도 했고 나름대로 적임자라고 생각합니다. 호텔리어가 되겠다고 결정한 순간부터 귀사에서 일하기를 희망해 왔습니다.

Q What do you know about our company / organization?
우리 회사에 대해 아는 것이 있습니까?

A I studied about your company and found that it has a great reputation. You offer good opportunities for promotions and take care of your employees and their family members. In addition, it offers a variety of cultural programs to the community and that way you are contributing to the culture and tourism of our city and country.

귀사에 대해 알아보았고 귀사가 좋은 평판을 가지고 있다고 들었습니다. 승진의 기회도 많고 직원을 가족같이 대우한다고 들었습니다. 귀사는 다양한 문화 프로그램을 지역주민들에게 제공하고, 지역사회 문화와 관광발전에 기여하고 있다고 알고 있습니다.

Q Why do you want to work for us?
왜 우리와 함께 일하고 싶습니까?

A I would like to have an opportunity to work in a hotel (or restaurant) and the work in your hotel would be a challenge to me. I need to learn about international standards. I'm sure that I can achieve that goal because your hotel (restaurant) is one of the world leading hotel / restaurant groups.

저는 호텔(또는 레스토랑)에서 일하고 싶고 귀사에서 일하는 것이 일종의 도전이 될 것으로 생각합니다. 호텔리어는 국제적인 표준을 배우고 싶어 합니다. 귀사는 세계적 호텔(레스토랑) 그룹의 선두주자에 속해 있으므로 많은 것을 배울 수 있는 기회가 되리라 봅니다.

Q What would you do if one of your guests was very upset?
손님이 화가 많이 났을 때 당신은 어떻게 하겠습니까?

A I think the first priority restaurant should be the guests, so I'll try to solve the problem which made him / her upset. When he/she goes too far, I'll persuade him/her to accept reasonable solutions.

먼저 손님이 왜 화가 났는지 알아보고 일단 손님을 진정시키는 것이 최우선이라고 생각합니다.
다만 무리한 요구를 하는 고객에게는 논리적으로 설득해 나가도록 하겠습니다.

Q Tell me about a big challenge or difficulty you've faced, how did you deal with it?

지금까지 살면서 겪었던 가장 어려운 문제는 무엇이었으며 어떻게 처리했습니까?

A (Answers vary.) When I worked part-time at the ○○Hotel, I had one guest who had gone to the airport forgetting his passport in his room. Since the passport is so important, I took a taxi to the airport for the guest to give it to him. He was very grateful and I felt proud of being a hotelier.

(개인 경험에 따라 답한다.) 제가 ○○호텔에서 아르바이트를 할 때, 고객이 여권을 두고 공항으로 가신 적이 있었습니다. 여권은 그 손님에게 아주 중요한 것이라서, 제가 택시를 타고 가서 직접 고객께 전달한 적이 있었습니다. 고객께서 매우 고마워하였습니다. 호텔리어의 보람을 찾았던 중요한 경험이었습니다.

Q Where do you see yourself in five years?

앞으로 5년 후에 당신은 어디에 있을 것으로 생각합니까?

A I see myself in the hospitality business and... well, I'll be a chef in charge of a culinary team. I'll be doing my best all the time and working with as much energy as I had as a novice worker. I'll train myself to be a good worker with a good command of foreign languages. I'll also cooperate with my colleagues for the job given to us.

저는 환대산업 분야에서 열심히 일하고 있을 것이며… 아마도 조리부의 책임자가 되어 있을 것입니다. 항상 초심을 유지하면서 전공과 외국어 실력을 쌓고, 대인관계를 넓혀서 많은 고객들과 동료직원들로부터 좋은 이미지를 받도록 노력하겠습니다.

Q What kind of experience have you had before?

어떤 경력이 있습니까?

A I had a part-time job on weekends at the ○○Hotel for 2 years. I worked at the cold kitchen most of the time and as a waiter for the last 6 months. I liked the work and the money I earned allowed me to be independent of my parents. It was a good job experience.

저는 ○○호텔에서 주말 아르바이트를 2년간 하였습니다. 주로 근무한 곳은 cold kitchen

이었고, 최근 6개월간은 웨이터로도 근무를 해본 적이 있습니다. 업무를 하나하나 익혀가는 재미가 있었고, 큰 돈은 아니지만 급여를 받아 저의 용돈은 부모님께 의존하지 않아도 되었습니다. 호텔의 아르바이트는 저의 성장과정에서 좋은 경험이라고 생각합니다.

Q What kind of specific tasks have you performed in your previous job?
전 직장에서는 어떤 구체적인 일을 하셨나요?
(본인이 경험한 주방 업무에 관하여 솔직하게 또한 구체적으로 말하라)

A The tasks I performed include washing, peeling and cutting various foods to prepare for cooking or serving. I even butcher and clean fowl, fish, poultry, and shellfish. I used to clean dishes, glasses, and tableware. I was also responsible for preparing special dressings and sauces as condiments for sandwiches, removing trash and cleaning kitchen garbage containers.
제가 한 일은 요리와 서빙을 준비하는 다양한 일 - 각종 재료를 씻는 일부터, 껍질 벗기기, 자르기 등이었습니다. 그릇, 유리제품, 식기류를 세척하기도 했습니다. 그리고 생선, 가금류, 어패류 등을 자르기도 했습니다. 또한 샌드위치용 드레싱이나 소스를 준비하기도 했고 쓰레기와 주방 쓰레기통 세척과 정리도 하였습니다.

Q What attracted you to this job?
왜 일에 매력을 느낍니까?

A I've hoped to be a hotelier for a long time and that's why I majored in culinary in college. I love to cook and meet people and I am happy when I see the customer I served happy. Being friendly is very important to a person who wants to be a businessman, a diplomat, or a serviceman. This is my one of my strengths and will be an asset to my future career.
저는 오랫동안 호텔리어가 되기를 희망해 왔고 그래서 대학에서 조리를 전공했습니다. 저는 요리하는 것과 사람 만나는 것을 좋아하고 제가 도와드린 손님이 행복해 하시면 저도 행복해집니다. 저는 사람을 잘 사귀는 장점을 가지고 있고, 이 때문에 늘 주변에 친구가 많았습니다. 사업, 외교, 관광업 등에 종사하려면 기본적으로 친화적인 성격을 갖는 것이 매우 중요하다고 보는데, 저의 장점을 살려 멋진 인생을 만들어갈 수 있을 것으로 봅니다.

Q When working with a group, do you tend to support or lead the team?

당신은 팀 구성원들과 일할 때 그 팀을 주도하는 편입니까? 아니면 도와주는 편입니까?

A I tend to support the team. Once a job is given to me, I do my best to complete the job. I believe that way I can contribute to the team.

저는 팀을 도와주는 편입니다. 저에게 일이 주어지면 저는 최선을 다해 그 일을 완성하려고 합니다. 저는 이런 방식으로 팀에 기여하고 싶습니다.

(혹은 이렇게 답할 수도 있다.)

It all depends. I support the team but I sometimes lead the team, too. I think that it is a matter of leadership. Teamwork works when each of the team members does his/her best, and at the same time takes the initiative and sets an example for others. I think I am a leader who takes the initiative and sets an example for others.

가끔은 도와주기도 하고, 제가 주도하기도 합니다. 무엇보다 중요한 것은 상황에 따라 도와주기도 하고, 주도하기도 하는 리더십이 중요하다고 인식하고 있습니다. 팀워크는 자기 희생에서 시작하고, 솔선수범하는 데서 발전하게 되지요. 저는 저 스스로가 솔선수범하는 서비스 리더라고 생각합니다.

Q How do you develop the trust of your team members?

어떻게 팀의 구성원들 사이에서 신뢰를 쌓겠습니까?

A I would try to listen to others speaking and to find out how I fit into the team. Words often hurt others, so I'll also be careful when I speak to my colleagues. If I am careful about my words and behavior, I think I can build up the trust of my team members. Another way would be to take the initiative and set an example for others, for example, being punctual for work and doing my best always.

저는 남의 말을 들으려고 하고 어떻게 하면 팀과 조화를 이룰 수 있을 것인가를 알아내도록 하겠습니다. 말로 자주 상대방을 상처받게 하는 경우가 있으므로 동료에게 말할 때에는 조심하도록 하겠습니다. 이렇게 제가 행동과 말을 조심하면 팀원 간에 신뢰를 쌓을 수 있을 것으로 생각합니다.

Q How would you deal with difficult customers or guests?
까다로운 손님을 어떻게 대하겠습니까?

A I'll try to find out how I can make the customer happy and be patient in any case. Customers are the most important asset to the hotel (restaurant). Only when we keep our word, we can keep the clientele. More than anything else, hotel (restaurant) staff should be aware of regulations and management policies, and stick to them. If we let the customers know about the services they deserve and take care of them, they are the keys solve any problems with customers.

까다로운 손님을 어떻게 하면 만족시킬 수 있을지를 알아내고 어떠한 경우에도 인내심을 가지고 모시겠습니다. 고객은 호텔 (레스토랑)의 자산입니다. 이들을 잘 유지하기 위해서는 호텔 (레스토랑)이 약속을 잘 지켜야 한다고 봅니다. 그러기 위해서는 직원들이 호텔 (레스토랑)의 규정과 경영방침을 정확하게 숙지하고 업무에 임해야 한다고 봅니다. 그것은 고객에게 각종 혜택을 친절하게 안내하고, 먼저 챙겨주는 업무습관에서 문제해결의 열쇠가 있다고 생각합니다.

Q How long do you think you'd stay with us if you were appointed?
우리 호텔/레스토랑에 고용되면 얼마동안 일할 수 있을 것으로 생각합니까?

A I applied to your company because your company has reasonable business policies and the potential to be the leading hotel in the hospitality (restaurant) industry. If I'm hired, I'll stay with this hotel as long as I can.

저는 귀사의 경영방향이 좋고, 성장 잠재력이 뛰어나기 때문에 지원을 하게 되었습니다. 만약 고용이 된다면 저는 귀 호텔/레스토랑과 함께 장기적으로 발전할 수 있도록 구체적인 계획을 세워 나갈 것입니다.

Q Do you have any special skills or interests?
특별한 기술이나 관심분야가 있습니까?

A Yes, I speak good English. I have a TOEIC score of 730 and a JLPT score of 460. I know how to use some computer softwares, such as Excel, word processing, and Power Point. I made my own homepage. I have a bartender's certificate and can make about 30 different cocktails. I also have a barista's certificate. Besides, I sometimes play the tennis.

저는 영어를 잘 구사합니다. 저는 영어 토익을 730점, 일어능력 시험에서 460점을 땄습니다. 그리고 컴퓨터는 엑셀, 워드, 한글, 파워포인트 등을 잘 구사할 수 있습니다. 가끔 저의 홈페이지를 만들기도 합니다. 바텐더 자격증을 가졌으며, 칵테일을 40여 종 만들 수 있고, 커피 바리스타 자격증도 보유하고 있습니다. 또한 저는 가끔 테니스도 칩니다.

Q Are you able to work flexible hours?
당신은 회사에서 요구하면 언제든지 출근해서 일할 수 있습니까?

A Yes, I am. If I'm hired, my job would be my first priority. When I had a part-time job, I used to work in the afternoon, but whenever I was asked to work extra hours, I worked from morning until late night. My house is close to your hotel, so I can work anytime when I am needed.

네, 그렇게 할 수 있습니다. 제가 취직이 되면 나의 일이 가장 중요한 일이 될 것입니다. 아르바이트를 할 때 주로 오후에 근무했었고, 바쁠 때는 오전에 출근하여 밤늦게 근무한 적도 있습니다. 이 호텔과 집이 가까워서 언제든지 출근할 수 있습니다.

※ 인터뷰를 마치고 나올 때 면접관에게 "Thank you"라고 말하는 것을 잊지 마라.

부 록

1. 서양요리 메뉴용어

agar agar 한천

agneau 양

aioli 프랑스식 마요네즈 소스. ail(마늘), oli(기름)가 기본이 되는 소스로 이태리어로 allioli,
스페인어로 aliolio라고 함

al dente 파스타나 채소를 조리할 때 쓰이는 용어로 씹었을 때 단단함이 느껴지는 정도

amande 아몬드

amandine 아몬드가 들어간

Americane 미국식

ananas 파인애플

anchois 앤초비

andalouse 토마토나 후추가 들어간

anglaise sauce 벨루테 소스에 노른자, 너트메그, 레몬즙이 첨가된 영국식 소스

anna Potato 감자를 얇게 슬라이스해서 밀가루를 뿌리고 동그란 모양으로 차곡차곡
쌓아 팬에 굽고 오븐에서 익힘

antipasto 전통적으로 파스타 먹기 전에 먹는 가벼운 형태의 음식으로 육류, 올리브,
치즈류, 각종 야채요리가 포함됨

aspic 돈육이나 가금육이 내포된 젤리성분. 찬 음식을 굳히거나 코팅을 위해 사용됨

aurore 벨루테 소스에 토마토 퓌레를 넣어 만든 응용소스

au beurre 버터가 들어간

au jus 고기육즙이 첨가된

au lait 우유가 들어간

à la carte 음식이나 음료의 가격이 각각 책정되어 적힌 메뉴

à la king 버섯, 양고추, 피망을 넣은 크림소스

à la parisíenne 파리식의

bain-marie 뜨거운 물이 조리된 음식이 담긴 용기를 넣어 따뜻하게 데우는 중탕기

baked alaska 케이크 위의 아이스크림

balsamic vinegar 이탈리아 에밀리아로마냐 지역, 모데나 시에서 처음으로 생산되었던 식초로 흰색의 트레비아노종 포도를 사용하여 농도가 생길 때까지 끓여준 후에 발효되지 않은 상태에서 주스를 숙성시켜 만든다. 오크통 속에서 10년간 숙성되면 색이 검게 변하게 되고, 증발되면 다시 작은 오크통으로 옮겨져 숙성과정을 거치게 된다.

barding 조리과정 동안 재료 표면이 건조되는 것을 방지하기 위해 버터, 오일, 소스를 끼얹거나 발라주는 것

barigoule 소를 넣고 브레이징한 아티초크 요리. 아티초크의 꼬리를 자르고 그릴에 구워 조리한 후 햄과 버섯을 다져서 아티초크 안에 소로 채워 넣어 브레이징함

baste 건조하게 구워지지 않게 하기 위해 소스나 버터를 발라주는 것

batonnet 프랑스어로 'Baton'은 '스틱'을 말하며 여기서 나온 용어로 추정된다. 알루미테(Allumette)나 쥘리엔느(Julienne)의 굵은 형태로 가로 1.5cm, 세로 1cm, 길이 5~6cm 정도의 크기로 써는 직사각형 형태

batter 튀김이나 머핀, 와플을 만들기 위한 되직한 반죽으로 밀가루에 물이나 우유, 달걀을 거품기로 저어 묽거나, 걸쭉한 형태

bavarois 요구르트나 크림에 젤라틴을 첨가해 틀에 넣어 만든 차가운 디저트

béarnaise 타라곤향이 첨가된 홀랜다이즈 응용소스

béchamel sauce 벨루테(veloute)에 우유를 넣은 백색의 크림소스로 정향(clove)을 양파에 꽂아 20~25분간 끓임

beignet 베녜는 튀김을 뜻하며 날것이나 익힌 재료에 반죽을 입혀 기름에 튀긴 요리로 프리터(Fritter)와 같은 의미

bercy sauce 파리의 베르시는 포도가 많이 경작되던 곳으로 1820년부터 어느 작은 레스토랑에서 포도주로 만들던 요리 이름이 그곳에서 유래되었다. 베르시 소스는 다진 샬롯에 화이트 와인과 벨루테를 넣어 조려서 만든 흰색 유지소스

bigarade sauce 비가라드 소스는 가금류 중 특히 오리고기 요리에 함께 제공되는 오렌지를 이용한 소스이다. 비가라드는 쓴맛을 내는 오렌지 나무의 일종이며 비가라드의 두꺼운 껍질 속 알맹이는 퀴라소 술을 만들 때 사용됨

bisque 비스큐는 스페인의 비스케 지방을 연상시키며 점차 조류를 이용한 비스크가 만들어졌고 17세기에는 갑각류(가재)가 주된 재료가 되었다. 새우(갑각류)의 껍질을 이용하여 양념하고 백포도주와 생크림을 첨가한 것으로 수프처럼 서비스됨

blanquette 백포도주를 곁들인 스튜

blintzes 크림치즈, 과일을 넣어 만 얇은 팬케이크

blue cheese 이탈리아 고르곤졸라 치즈와 프랑스의 로케포르 치즈, 영국의 스틸턴 치즈 는 블루치즈이다. 로케포르 치즈는 양의 우유를 사용하며, 고르곤졸라는 황소의 우유를 사용하여 맛이 부드럽고 크리미하다. 스틸턴 치즈는 영국에서 생산되며 잘 숙성되고 부서지기 쉬운 거친 질감을 가지며 향이 매우 강함

bombe 둥근 덩어리로 뭉친 아이스크림

bordelaise sauce 프랑스 북부 보르도의 대표적인 적포도주 소스. 샬롯과 마늘을 버 터에 볶다가 적포도주를 넣고 1/2로 조린 다음 타임과 월계수잎, 브라운 소스를 넣고 1시간 정도 끓임

borsch 채소를 큼직하게 썰어서 만든 북유럽의 전통적인 수프

bouillabaisse 어패류, 사프란, 와인, 토마토를 넣어 만든 프랑스 남부의 생선스튜

bouilli 끓인

bouilon 맑은 수프

bouquetiere 야채를 혼합한

bouquet garni 셀러리, 파슬리줄기, 월계수잎, 타임, 통후추 등을 실로 묶어 스톡, 수프, 소스, 스튜 등에 넣어 잡냄새를 제거하고 향을 살리기 위해 첨가됨

brochettes 꼬챙이에 끼워 구운 고기

brunoise style 작은 다이스 형태. 표준형은 3mm의 크기의 정육면체로 써는 것. 콩소 메, 테린, 장식으로 사용됨

bruschetta 이탈리아 안티파스터로 오픈 샌드위치 형태이며 빵 위에 토마토와 아스파 라거스, 육회, 프로슈토햄 등의 재료를 사용

canape 작은 조각의 빵이나 과자 위에 다양한 재료를 올려 한입 크기로 만든 요리

canard 오리

cardinal sauce 베샤멜 소스에 트러플과 로브스터를 넣어 만든 응용소스

carpaccio 얼린 쇠고기나 생선을 얇게 썬 것으로 식초가 첨가된 소스와 신선한 야채와 함께 제공되는 요리이다. 원래 카르파치오는 고유명사로 이탈리아 베네치아의 유명 한 Harry's Bar의 단골손님이었던 카르파치오(Carpaccio)라는 추상화가가 유난히 육회요리를 좋아했다고 해서 붙여진 이름

carry-over cooking 여열조리법. 열원을 제거한 후에도 재료에 남아 있는 내부의 열에

의해 조리가 계속 이어지는 것

carte de jour 그날의 메뉴

casserole 밥, 감자 또는 수분이 있는 음식을 조리할 수 있는 바닥이 두꺼운 팬으로 오븐의 높은 열에도 견딜 수 있는 냄비

caul 동물의 위와 내장을 둘러싸고 있는 지방질이나 막

caviar 캐비어는 철갑상어의 알을 가공한 식품으로 미국산은 본래 깡통째로, 한 면은 버터를 바른 토스트, 레몬, 양념을 하여 간 양파, 삶은 계란의 흰자와 노른자를 따로 다진 것, 사워크림과 함께 먹거나 토스트 대신 딱딱한 빵이나 크래커를 사용할 수도 있다. 질이 떨어지는 캐비어는 소스나 토핑의 재료로 사용하거나 사워크림과 혼합해서 사용한다.

caviare 러시아나 폴란드, 우크라이나 등 북유럽에서 사용되는 것. 조리된 야채로부터 만들어지는 스프레드나 딥

cèpe 다양한 버섯

chantilly cream 바닐라향의 거품을 많이 낸 크림

chaud 뜨거운

chaud-froid 데미글라스를 이용한 갈색소스, 허브를 이용한 녹색소스, 토마토를 이용한 붉은색 소스, 베샤멜 소스를 이용한 흰색의 소스로 뜨겁거나 차게 제공되는 전통적인 코팅소스를 의미한다. 자주 사용되지는 않지만 카나페와 오르되브르, 접시 장식을 위한 중요한 소스로 맑은 코팅소스는 콩소메를 이용하여 만든 아스픽 젤리임

chervil 부드러운 녹색 잎을 가진 허브로 생선요리와 샐러드와 야채, 계란요리에 매우 많이 사용된다. 매우 부드러운 풍미를 갖고 있으며 파슬리와 아니스의 향을 연상시킴

chili oil 매콤한 맛을 내기 위해 사용되는 기름으로 중국요리나 태국요리에 파기름과 함께 사용되는 기름

chowder 대합, 생선, 감자 등의 재료가 듬뿍 들어간 걸쭉한 크림 수프

chutney 신선하고, 달콤하고, 양념을 많이 한 다진 야채와 과일로 만듦

cider vinegar 사과로 만든 식초로 와인식초와 몰트식초의 중간 맛을 띤다. 신선한 토마토와 함께 사용하면 풍미가 증가됨

citrus 오렌지, 자몽, 레몬 등의 유자류

compote 삶은 과일

compote 신선하거나 말린 과일을 통째로 혹은 조각내어 농축된 시럽에 담가서 만든

음식

compound butter 부드럽게 한 버터에 허브나 마늘 등을 넣어 만든 것

condiment 캐비어 콘디멘트는 삶은 달걀, 양파, 레몬, 차이브이며, 훈제연어 콘디멘트
는 케이퍼, 호스래디시, 양파, 레몬, 삶은 달걀임

confit 오리, 거위, 또는 마늘 등을 기름에 재워 낮은 온도에서 오랫동안 조리하는 것

coq au vin 닭을 적당한 크기로 잘라 색을 낸 후에 포도주를 첨가하여 조려 조리한
프랑스식 닭요리

corned beef 소금물에 절인 쇠고기로 미국식 아침식사에서 해시 감자를 넣고 볶아 계
란요리와 함께 제공

coulis 밀가루를 첨가하지 않고 야채나 과일을 퓌레 형태로 만든 것으로 과거에는 생
선이나 고기의 퓌레 용액을 말한다. 에스코피에의 저서 <Le Guide Culinaire>에
서는 "쿨리란 잘 졸여지고 음식의 필수적인 향을 전체적으로 잘 함유하고 갈아져
수분의 형태를 띠고 있는 것"이라 하였다.

court bouillon 문자 그대로 해석하면 '짧게 끓인 브로스'로 향이 풍부한 야채 브로스
에는 신맛의 성분(와인, 식초)이 포함되며 보통 생선을 삶기 위해 준비하는 육수

crepe 우유에 밀가루를 첨가하여 팬에 얇게 구운 전병으로 안에 각종 과일을 첨가하
거나 치즈 등을 첨가

crûton 식빵을 주사위 꼴로 썰어 팬에 토스트하거나 버터에 튀겨낸 빵조각으로 수프,
샐러드에 곁들임

cuisine 프랑스, 스위스, 미국과 같은 서양에서의 요리(조리방식)를 의미함

curing 소금에 절이거나 훈제, 건조, 초절임과 같이 식품을 저장하는 방법

curing salt 94%의 소금(Sodium chloride)과 6%의 아질산염(Nitrite)인 T.C.M으로
육류나 소시지의 색을 선명하게 살려주는 착색제 및 방부제. 식용으로 사용 시 법
적 규제량에 따라 제한함

depouillage 스톡이나 스톡 등의 조리과정 중에 위로 떠오르는 불순물을 제거하는 것

devil 겨자향이나 매운맛이 나도록 조미하는 것. 겨자향이 나는 요리

distilled vinegar 물처럼 투명하며 원재료의 색을 살리기 위한 음식 절임에 사용되는
증류식초. 향이 매우 강하고 점차 술처럼 되어감

doyley pepper 패스트리, 케이크 등을 싸거나 바닥에 받치는 용도의 종이로 바닥에

붙지 않고 위생적인 처리를 하기 위함

dubarry 콜리플라워가 들어 있거나 콜리플라워로 장식한 것

dusting 밀가루, 설탕, 코코아 가루 등을 팬이나 완성된 음식 위에 얇게 뿌리는 것

duxelles 잘게 썬 버섯류와 샬롯을 버터에 소테한 후 비프 웰링턴 같은 음식 속에 넣거나 장식성을 살리기 위해 스테이크 위에 뿌리기도 함

egg wash 달걀물

encasserole 개인 접시에 서비스하는

enchilladas 옥수수 토르티야 안에 멕시코 고추와 야채, 닭고기, 치즈 등을 말아서 만든 멕시코 전통요리로 토마토소스와 치즈를 뿌려 만듦

entrecote 미국에서는 Sirloin Steak로 익히 사용되며, '갈비 사이에'라는 뜻

entree 메인디시

entremets 달콤한, 디저트

en papillote 유선지 백에 넣어 굽는

epinard 시금치

escargots 달팽이

farce 간 고기

farci ~을 꽉 채운

fillet 뼈 없는 육류

fish sauce 남아시아와 동아시아에서는 테이블에 있는 소금을 음식에 넣어 조미하는 것과 같은 방법으로 사용한다. 생선을 절여서 발효시킨 맑은 액체상태의 소스로 자극적인 향과 짠맛이 강하다. 태국에서는 남 피아(nam pia), 필리핀에서는 파티스(patis), 베트남에서는 누옥 맘(nuoc mam)으로 불리며 다양한 음식과 혼합되며 찍어 먹음

flambe 불꽃의

flavored oil 음식의 전체적인 맛을 내기 위한 용도의 기름으로 향신료와 스파이스, 선드라이드 토마토 또는 레몬 껍질 같은 재료를 오일에 넣어 만든다. 대부분의 사용 용도는 파스타와 샐러드에 집중됨

flavored vinegar 향초식초는 신선한 허브(타라곤, 민트, 바질 등)를 병에 담아 냉장고
에서 24~36시간 동안 흔들지 말고 공기가 통하지 않게 보관한다. 보관시간이 되
면 체에 걸러 다양한 음식에 첨가가능

florentine 시금치를 곁들인

foie-gras 프랑스어로 푸아(Foie)는 '간', 그라(Gras)는 '비대한'의 뜻으로 푸아그라는
비대한 간을 말하며, 주로 가금류인 거위와 오리의 간을 일컫는다. 푸아그라는 기름
지면서도 부드럽고, 씹힐 듯 하면서도 씹히지 않고 입에서 녹아드는 독특한 육질로,
테린이나 파테처럼 고급음식에 이용되기도 하며, 날것을 그대로 구워 먹기도 함

foie de veau 송아지 간

fond 스톡

fricassee 닭고기, 송아지고기 등을 잘게 썰어 버섯과 함께 볶은 것에 화이트소스를 첨
가하여 만든 요리

fromage 치즈

galantine 프랑스혁명(1789~1799) 이후 '젤리'를 뜻하는 고대 프랑스어 'Gelatine'으로
사용되었으나, 오늘날 갤런틴(Galantine)으로 정착하였으며 닭을 의미한다. 갤런틴
은 대부분 닭, 오리, 꿩 같은 가금류의 뼈를 발라낸 상태에서 포스미트를 채워 원
통 형태로 말아 스톡에 넣고 끓여 차게 제공하는 요리

garde-manger 찬 요리 주방

garfrette 와플모양으로 자르는 방법

garnish 요리에 장식효과를 내기 위해 첨가되는 먹을 수 있는 아이템

gateau 스펀지에 잼을 바른 후 크림을 바르고 샌드하여 스펀지를 놓고 위에 초콜릿이
나 퐁당을 씌운 케이크

gelatin 동물이나 생선의 뼈나 가죽, 힘줄, 내장 등에 포함되어 있는 콜라겐(collagen)
이 주요 성분으로 정제도가 높고 투명한 양질의 젤라틴은 식용으로 사용되고 있으며
무향, 무미, 무취, 무 칼로리의 특성을 갖는다. 불순물이 포함된 저질의 젤라틴은
아교(glue)라 하며 공업용으로 사용됨

gnocchi 삶은 감자에 밀가루, 세몰리나 등을 섞어 반죽하여 모양을 낸 작은 크기의 파
스타 종류

gofard sauce 양파와 다진 마늘을 버터에 넣어 볶다가 햄을 넣고 글라스 드 비앙드를

넣어 살짝 끓인 소스

goulash 파프리카로 조리하여 뭉근히 끓인 쇠고기 또는 송아지고기

gravelax 그라브락스는 스칸디나비아식으로 처리된 연어로 lax(스웨덴어)로 표기하든
　　　　laks(덴마크어와 노르웨이어), lachs(독일어)나 lox(이디시어 : 독일어에 슬라브어와
　　　　히브리어를 섞어 히브리문자로 쓰며, 유럽과 미국의 유대인 사이에서 주로 쓰임)로
　　　　표기하든 그 뜻은 연어이며 'Gravelax'는 땅에 묻은 연어라는 뜻이다. 연어는 2장
　　　　뜨기 해서 뼈를 발라내고 트리밍한 후에 소금, 설탕, 후추, 브랜디, 딜 등으로 절여
　　　　냉장고에서 12시간 보관한 후에 다시 연어를 뒤집어 2~3일 후에 사용한다. 애피
　　　　타이저나 카나페 등의 고급요리에 사용

griddle 약 0.7cm 되는 두꺼운 철판 위에서 재료를 볶는 것

grill 육류나 생선 등을 뜨겁게 달궈진 석쇠에 올려놓고 직화로 굽는 기구

haggis 송아지나 면양의 간과 심장, 폐를 이용하여 만든 스코틀랜드 전통요리

hors d'oeuvres 파티나 리셉션에서 제공되는 한입 크기의 작은 음식

joinville 포치(Poach)한 생선에 소스를 뿌린 혀가자미 요리의 명칭

joinville sauce 크림과 계란노른자를 넣어 진하게 하고 버섯 에센스, 굴즙, 그리고 작
　　　　은 새우와 가재 쿨리로 장식된 혀가자미 벨루테로 만든다. 또한 여러 가지 모양으
　　　　로 간소화되기도 하는데 브레이징한 생선요리와 관계있는 경우 가재 버터와 쥘리
　　　　엔느로 썬 송로버섯이 첨가된 새우소스, 혹은 작은 새우 버터가 첨가된 노르망디소
　　　　스로 만들기도 함

laddy curzon 콩소메 위에 크림을 휘핑한 뒤 커리향을 첨가하여 그라탱한 요리

larding 기름기가 없는 고깃덩어리에 돼지비계를 가늘고 길게 썰어서 고깃덩어리 표면
　　　　에 꿰매 붙여 넣는 것을 말함. 이렇게 하면 고기에 수분이 유지되고 맛이 향상됨

lyonnaise 프랑스 리옹 지방식 요리로 요리에 양파의 맛과 향이 강하게 나도록 양파를
　　　　넣어 만든 요리

malt vinegar 맥아식초는 보리를 양조하여 만들어진다. 갈색의 캐러멜색을 갖고 있고 최고의 상품은 초절임에 사용된다. 또한 영국의 유명한 음식인 'Fish & Chips'에 곁들임

marinade 조리 전 육류나 어류의 풍미를 좋게 하고 육질을 부드럽게 하기 위한 목적으로 사용되는 절임의 의미이며 중요한 조리과정을 말한다. 건조한 상태에서나 절임액으로도 사용된다. 육류 및 어류 등에도 풍부한 맛을 첨가하기 위해 부드러운 육질에도 사용된다. 육류는 오일을 기초로 사용되며 신맛이 나는 액체 등에도 이용된다. 조리하기 전에 제거하고 사용될 수도 있으며 용액을 함께 사용할 수도 있음

meat loaf 갈은 육류에 크래커나 빵가루, 계란 등을 함께 섞어 덩어리로 만들어 구운 것을 의미한다. 오븐에 중탕으로 구워 만든 것으로 뜨겁게 먹지만, 작게 잘라 찬 오르되브르에 사용하기도 함

melba toast 통 식빵을 얇게 슬라이스하여 여러 형태로 자른 후 오븐에 구워 바삭하게 한 것으로 생선요리에 함께 제공되며 서양식 육회 같은 다짐요리(tartare)에는 필수적으로 동반됨

meringue 계란흰자에 설탕을 첨가하고 빽빽하게 거품낸 것. 익히는 정도에 따라 거품이 있거나 바삭바삭하다. 머랭은 보통머랭, 이태리머랭, 머랭 쉬르르푀(meringue sur le feu)가 있음

meuniere 팬에 볶아 갈색버터와 함께 서비스하는

mirepoix 스톡, 수프, 브레이징, 스튜잉 등의 향미를 내기 위한 양파, 당근, 셀러리

mise-en-place 적소에 위치한다는 뜻으로 조리준비에 필요한 제반 준비작업을 조리 전에 마무리하여 끝내 놓는 것을 의미

monte au beurre 소스에 깊은 맛을 더하고 부드럽고 윤기나게 하기 위해 소스 마지막 단계에서 버터를 넣는 것

mould 틀, 형, 주형

mousse 거품낸 크림

mousseline 홀랜다이즈 소스에 휘핑한 크림을 넣어 만든 응용소스

naan(nan) 난이라는 빵은 Naan 또는 Nan으로 표기되는 동인도의 주요한 탄수화물 급

원으로 밀가루와 요구르트로 반죽되고 공기 중의 자연적인 이스트에 의해 부풀려진다. 이 빵은 전통적으로 탄두리(tandoori : 인도의 화로)에서 굽는다. 반죽은 피자처럼 아주 납작하게 만들어 탄두리라는 화로에 붙여 구워진다. 몇 초가 되지 않아 빵은 살짝 부풀고 곧이어 색이 남

napper style 소스를 요리 표면 전체에 뿌리는 방법

newbury 베샤멜소스 같은 크림소스류에 백포도주와 달걀노른자를 넣은 것

niçoise 프랑스 니스 지역식 요리

noisette 헤이즐넛 또는 헤이즐넛 색상의 육류나 채소를 작고 둥글게 깎는 방법

nougar 끓인 설탕에 아몬드 슬라이스를 넣어 반죽상태로 만든 것과 이것을 부셔서 초콜릿을 혼합한 것

nouille 국수

nouvelle cuisine 버터의 양을 최소화하며 맛도 가볍게 하고 조리과정 중에 때로는 새로운 배합(동양의 식재료)도 과감하게 사용하면서 조리하는 새로운 형태의 프랑스식 조리법

pain 빵

parcooking 재료를 완전히 익히지 않고 반쯤만 조리하는 것

pâté 육류나 생선을 곱게 다져 양념하여 차게 한 것

paupiette '작은 상품'이라는 뜻으로 야채를 쥘리엔느로 썰고 실파 등을 함께 넣어 다발을 만들어 생선 살 안에 넣고 마는 것

pesto 올리브유에 바질, 앤초비, 마늘을 함께 갈아 만든 이탈리아 소스

piccata 송아지고기를 얇게 저며 썰어 계란물에 담가 그리들에 구운 것

pumpernikel 호밀을 거칠게 빻아 만든 빵

quenelle 돼지나 생선 등을 이용한 포스미트를 스푼을 이용하여 타원형의 모양으로 만든 것을 의미한다. 콩소메 같은 값비싼 수프의 가니쉬로 사용하지만, 일반적으로는 맛이나 질감을 평가하기 위해 맛을 보기 위한 차원에서 사용

raft 콩소메를 맑게 하기 위해 사용되는 재료들을 혼합하는 것

ratatouille 프랑스 프로방스 지역에서 일상적으로 먹는 야채 스튜요리로 알려져 있지만, 원래 니스 지역이 원산지로 사전적으로는 '맛없는 스튜'를 뜻하는 좋지 않은 의미로 사용되었다. 야채의 섭취를 위한 건강식 요리로 가지, 호박, 양파, 토마토, 토마토 페이스트 등을 올리브유에 넣어 만든 음식

rice pepper 미분, 소금, 물로 만들어지고 죽순으로 만든 매트(mats) 위에서 태양열을 이용하여 말린다. 라이스페이퍼는 둥그런 모양이나 큰 직사각형 모양으로 이용되며 스프링롤과 다른 음식을 말기 위해 이용된다. 얇은 시트는 사용 전 더운물에 몇 초 동안 담갔다가 사용한다.

라이스페이퍼를 이용한 대표적인 음식은 동남아의 포피아(Poh Piah)임

rice vinegar 쌀을 이용한 식초는 주로 일본과 남-서쪽의 아시아에서 사용됨. 특히 초밥을 지을 때 사용되는 식초

rosette 장미꽃 모양의 장식을 말하며, 꽃모양의 매듭을 의미하기도 한다.

roti 구운

rouille 껍질 벗긴 붉은색 피망과 빵, 마늘, 토마토, 올리브유를 넣고 부드럽게 갈아서 프렌치 브레드를 얹어 제공되는 요리. 프로방스 지역의 요리로 부야베스라는 수프에 곁들임

roux 녹인 버터와 밀가루를 섞은 혼합물로서 수프와 소스를 되직하게 하기 위한 농밀제

sachet d'épices 작은 치즈클로스(muslin) 안에 타임, 파슬리 줄기, 월계수잎, 마늘, 통후추를 넣은 향신료 묶음. 스톡과 쿠르부용에 향을 주기 위함

salsa 살사는 익히지 않은 과일이나 야채를 이용하여 만드는 멕시코 소스

samosa 인도 거리에서 판매하는 리어카나 노점음식인 스낵의 일종. 얇은 밀가루전병에 고기나 야채를 넣어 삼각형 모양으로 말아 기름에 튀긴 요리

sauerbraten 독일의 전통요리로 쇠고기를 식초와 레드와인으로 절여 놓았다가 끓인 음식

sauerkraut 양배추를 썰어 소금으로 간을 하여 절여 놓았다가 베이컨과 함께 볶아 소시지와 함께 먹는 독일식 김치

saumon 연어

searing 그리들이나 브로일러, 혹은 프라이팬에 높은 온도(열)를 가하여 고기 표면을 갈색을 내어 육즙의 유출을 막기 위한 조리방법이다. 육류나 생선 로스팅 전의 조리과정에 있어 필수적인 단계

sherry vinegar 스페인산 백포도주에서 얻어지는 식초로 부드럽게 숙성된 것은 발사믹 식초를 대신할 정도로 주방에서 최고의 가치를 가질 수 있다. 레몬주스와 섞어 비네그레트를 만들면 견과류 맛이 나는데 거의 호두 오일과 비슷하다. 프랑스의 셰프들은 이 식초를 병아리 식초(Poulet au vinaigre)라 부름

spatzle 밀가루 반죽을 사용하여 만들 수 있는 짧은 모양의 국수

strain 액체를 고운체 등으로 걸러냄

tabbouleh 으깬 밀에 향료, 토마토, 야채 등을 넣고 올리브유와 레몬즙을 첨가하여 버무린 서아시아, 지중해 지역의 음식. 으깬 밀 대신 쿠스쿠스를 사용하며 서브할 때는 다진 붉은 양파와 신선한 박하잎을 함께 섞음

table d'hôte 다양한 코스를 지정된 가격으로 선택할 수 있는 음식

tapenade 타프나드는 전통적으로 프랑스의 프로방스 사람들이 케이퍼, 앤초비, 마늘을 다져 올리브유와 함께 절여 만든 스프레드의 일종임. 재료는 으깬 페이스트 상태로 만들어 피자와 빵에 바르거나 생야채를 위한 딥으로 사용됨

tasse 컵

terrine 사전적으로 '항아리에 넣어서 보존한 고기'라는 뜻으로 고전적으로 양념된 포스미트는 혼합하고 단단한 뚜껑이 있는 그릇 틀 안에 넣어 중탕해 조리함. 스테인리스, 알루미늄, 세라믹, 에나멜을 입힌 무쇠, 오븐에 사용 가능한 플라스틱 또는 윤이 난 것으로 모양이 다양함

timbal 팀발(Timbal)은 아라비어에서 파생된 말로, 작은 음료를 먹을 수 있는 드럼(Drum: Tahbal) 모양의 컵을 지칭한다. 전통적으로 주인은 손님을 초대하였을 때 팀발에 식전주(Aperitif Beverage)를 가득 채워 제공함

tomato concasse 토마토껍질을 벗겨 작은 다이스형태로 써는 것. 다양한 음식의 장식

tortillas 토르티야는 멕시코의 빵이다. 옥수수나 호밀가루로부터 만들어지고 둥그렇고

얇은 모양이다. 토르티야는 항상 뜨겁게 제공되며 빵은 바구니에 담겨 나오는데 이 토르티야로 접시에 묻어 있는 소스를 깨끗하게 닦아서 먹는 모습을 볼 수 있다. 미국인들은 그것을 스팀하거나 튀기는 형태로 만들고 토르티야는 타코(taco), 엔칠라다(Enchilladas), 케사디야(Quesadillas), 토스타다(Tostadas)와 비슷한 요리들을 준비하기 위한 기초재료로 사용된다.

truffle 관세 품목상 송로버섯으로 분류되어 있으나, 소나무와는 아무 관계가 없고 실제는 주로 떡갈나무 숲의 땅속에서 자라며, 개나 돼지의 예민한 후각을 이용하여 캐냄. 땅속에서 채취하여 식물의 뿌리로 생각하기 쉽지만 식물분류학상 엄연히 버섯류에 속함

truffle oil 트러플에서 추출된 최고급 오일로 모든 요리에 소량씩 사용한다. 장기간 보관이 가능하므로 소량씩 사용하며 이탈리아의 스튜요리와 버섯요리에 주로 사용됨

veal 송아지고기

velouté 생선, 닭, 송아지 육수로 만든 화이트 소스

vichyssoise 감자와 파로 끓여 만든 찬 수프

vin 포도주

vinaigre 식초

vol au vent 직경 2cm 정도 되는 작은 빵(puff pastry shell)으로 안쪽 윗부분은 칼로 도려내어 뚜껑으로 사용하고, 그 안에 뜨거운 내용물을 채워 넣는다.

walnut oil 많은 양의 호두를 압착해서 추출한 오일로 풍미가 좋아 특별한 샐러드에 사용

watercress 유럽 중남부가 원산지로 우리나라 이름으로 물냉이, 양갓냉이, 후추풀이라고도 하며 향긋하면서도 톡 쏘는 쌉쌀한 매운맛의 채소이다. 크레송이라고도 하며 비타민 A는 상추의 20배, 비타민 C는 11배나 되며 비타민 B_{19}를 함유한다. 항암작용이 있어 건강식의 녹즙이나 드레싱으로 활용

wellington 파이반죽 안에 안심, 거위간 또는 뒥셀(duxelles)을 넣고 말아 오븐에서 구운 요리

zamponi 돼지 족발의 살에 야채와 다진 고기를 채워 넣은 이태리의 전통요리
zest 유자류의 껍질을 얇게 채 썬 것

2. 식음재료 이동 인수증(Inter Kitchen, Bar Transfer)

| | | | | | | FBC-6/20 |

Seoul Hilton

식음재료 이동 인수증

INTER- ☐ KITCHEN TRANSER
☐ BAR

DATE _____

FROM _____

TO _____

FOR _____

Q'TY ORDERED	UNIT	ARTICLE & DESCRIPTION	Q'TY OR WT-ISSUED	UNIT COST	AMOUNT
		TOTAL COST			

_____ _____ _____ _____
ORDERED BY   ISSUED BY   RECEIVED BY   HEAD OF DEPT

자료제공 : 서울힐튼호텔

3. 창고물건불출증(Store Requisition)

창 고 물 건 불 출 증
STORES   REQUISITION

Seoul Hilton

| FOOD | ☐ | GENERAL | ☐ | No. 24870 |
| BEVERAGE | ☐ | OTHERS | ☐ | |

DEPT.: _____   DATE: _____

QUAN.	UNIT	DESCRIPTION	CODE No.	QUAN. ISSUED	UNIT PRICE	AMOUNT

(ORDERED BY)	(APROVED BY)	(ISSUED BY)	(RECEIVED BY)

자료제공 : 서울힐튼호텔

4. 해외조리인턴십 지원양식

APPLICATION

(PLEASE TYPE OR PRINT CLEARLY IN BLACK INK. CHECK BOXES WHERE APPROPRIATE. **PRINT NAME EXACTLY IT APPEARS ON YOUR PASSPORT**)

Family Name:	First Name:	Middle Name:	
Date of Birth(mm/dd/yyyy):	Gender: Male ☐ Female ☐		**Attach photo here.** *Smile!*
City of Birth:	Country of Birth:		
Country of Legal Permanent Residency:	Country of Citizenship:(Country issuing passport)		

APPLICANT CURRENT CONTACT INFOMATION

Applicant Email Address: (required)	
Phone Number 1: Country Code City code phone Number	Phone Number 2: Country Code City code phone Number
Your Present Mailing Address:	
City: Country: Postal Code:	

APPLICANT'S EMERGENCY CONTACT INFORMATION (Your emergency contact must speak English and cannot be your attorney)

Emergency contact Name:	Relationship to Applicant:
Emergency contact Phone Number 1 : Country Code City code phone Number	Emergency contact Phone Number 2 : Country Code City code phone Number
Emergency Contact Email Address:	

EDUCATION	Name of School	Course of school	Dates attended	Diploma or Degree Received
Secondary School				
College/University (1)				
College/University (2)				
Graduate Work				
Vocational/Trade school				

Hotelintern.com I CareerTraining Application

3FL. Hanyang B/D. 1-139 Dongsoong-dong
Jongno-gu. Seoul. 110-809. Korea
TEL : +82(0)2.717.8526 / FAX : +82(0)2.3673.5339

자료제공 : 호텔인턴닷컴

참고문헌

김정혜(2007). 간호취업영어. 정담미디어.

루이스 이구아라스(2011). 요리학교에서 배운 101가지. 동녘.

엘리류(2004). JOB 아라 취업영어. 넥서스.

윤석환·피터천(2012). 취업대비세트. 스피쿠스.

이지윤(2007). 취업영어 50 KEY POINT. YBMSISA.

이형필(2008). 취업영어인터뷰. 학문사닷컴.

이희천(1993). Everyday college & travel english. 문운당.

장 호(2009). 취업영어면접. 서원각.

한영주 외(2010). 호텔영어 1000문장 익히기(개정판). 도서출판 대명.

Hyo Jin Kim & Chole Y Kim(2011). 조리실무영어. 기린원.

Mitsuyo Arimoto/남상현 역(2004). 인터뷰영어. 인터원.

Ayla Esen Algar(1996). The Complete Book of Turkish Cooking.

Jean Reed(2002). Resumes that Get Jobs. Arco.

Keith Harding & Paul Henderson(1995). High Season. Oxford University Press.

Lawrence J. Zwier(2006). Everyday English for Hospitality Professionals. Compass
    Publishing.

M. Swan & C. Walter(2003). The Good Grammar Book with Answers. Oxford
    University Press.

Raymond Murphy & William R. Smalzer(2011). Basic Grammar in Use. 2nd
    Edition. Cambridge.

Rebecca Hayden(1956). Mastering American English. Prentice Hall.

Renee Talalla(2008). English for Restaurant Workers. Compass Publishing.

Ruth Wajnryb(2000). Travel and Tourism. MacMillan Languagehouse.

Susan Ireland(2010). The Complete Idiot' Guide to the Perfect Resume. Alpha
    Books.

서울힐튼호텔. 식재료이동인수증 및 창고물건불출증.

한식메뉴외국어표기안(2009). 농림수산식품부.

Hotelintern.com. Career Training Application.

참고 사이트

http://www.foodreference.com/html/crosswords.html

1. Crosswords, Meat # 1 재작성
2. Crosswords, Sauce # Ⅰ1 재작성
3. Crosswords, Sauce # Ⅱ2 재작성
4. Crosswords, Fruit # 1 재작성
5. Crosswords, Drink 재작성
6. Crosswords, Soup # 1 재작성
7. Crosswords, Herb & Spice # 1 재작성
8. Crosswords, Meat # 1 재작성

(표지사진 제공 : 호텔인턴닷컴)

▌저자소개

고범석

대구보건대학교 호텔외식조리학부 교수 / Ph. D.
전, (주)대우개발 서울힐튼호텔

김민영

미국 피츠버그대학교 대학원 / 영어교육학 전공
전, 웨스틴조선호텔 및 파라다이스호텔 마케팅 실장

나태균

두원공과대학교 호텔조리과 교수 / Ph. D.
전, (주)아시안스타 메뉴개발팀 팀장, 조리기능장

글로벌조리실무영어

2014년 5월 10일 초판 1쇄 발행
2021년 2월 20일 초판 3쇄 발행

지은이 고범석 · 김민영 · 나태균
펴낸이 진욱상
펴낸곳 백산출판사
교 정 편집부
본문디자인 편집부
표지디자인 오정은

저자와의
합의하에
인지첩부
생략

등 록 1974년 1월 9일 제406-1974-000001호
주 소 경기도 파주시 회동길 370(백산빌딩 3층)
전 화 02-914-1621(代)
팩 스 031-955-9911
이메일 edit@ibaeksan.kr
홈페이지 www.ibaeksan.kr

ISBN 978-89-6183-946-4 93740
값 22,000원